1.00

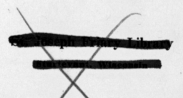

THE HEART OF CHRIST

BY JEAN GALOT, S.J.

THE HEART
OF CHRIST

TRANSLATED BY JOHN CHAPIN

THE NEWMAN PRESS · WESTMINSTER, MD.
1955

Nihil obstat: EDWARD A. CERNY, S.S., D.D.
Censor Librorum

Imprimatur: FRANCIS P. KEOUGH, D.D.
Archbishop of Baltimore

March 2, 1955

The *nihil obstat* and *imprimatur* are official declarations that a book
or pamphlet is free of doctrinal and moral error. No implication is
contained therein that those who have granted the *nihil obstat* and
imprimatur agree with the opinions expressed.

ACKNOWLEDGMENT

The Scripture translations throughout are from the translation of Monsignor Ronald Knox: the *Old Testament*, Volume I, copyright 1948; the *Old Testament*, Volume II, copyright 1950; the *New Testament*, copyright 1944, by Sheed and Ward, Inc., New York.

INTRODUCTION

The object of our study is to discover the intimate thoughts of Jesus as they are described or suggested by the Gospels and to penetrate the heart of the God-Man. Christ continues to live in his Church and in Christian souls; he secretly converses with hearts and reveals himself in what he says. He may be studied in the light of what the great mystics have taught about him or what has been privately revealed, but nothing can give us a better idea of Christ than a study of his public revelation as this has been preserved for us in the Gospels. That was the way he offered himself to all men, and the Gospels are the means whereby the light of the Holy Spirit makes him appear to us in all his profound mystery.

The Evangelists were not particularly concerned with the depths of Christ's heart. Their purpose was to describe the principal events of his life from an objective and purely external point of view. They fortunately refrained from indulging in psychological analysis and were divinely inspired to be mere witnesses. While carefully preserving the letter of their writings, the Church invites us to ponder over the meaning of what they wrote and has no wish to confine us to a perfunctory and uninspired interpretation of the pages of Holy Scripture. The One who originally inspired the authors of those pages will also inspire the Christian reader today to discover the hidden treasure which lies buried in them. We shall try to penetrate rather deeply into the secret recesses of Christ's soul, to discover the reasons for his various acts and attitudes, and to reach the very core of his activity, the living water of his love. Both the broad purpose and the most insignificant details in his life are explained in terms of love; his whole life is summed up in love; his heart is the key to his whole personality, because it is the seat of his love.

CONTENTS

THE HEART OF CHRIST

1. HEART TURNED TOWARD THE FATHER

I live because of the Father

In the life of Christ one concept seems to dominate all his thoughts and feelings like an obsession: the Father. The heart of Christ is above all the heart of a Son, the most loving of sons. The Gospel of St. John, which portrays the heart of Christ in greatest detail, is also the one in which his concern for the Father appears to predominate. In reading this Gospel we realize that Jesus lives by means of his love for the Father; this love forms the basis for his whole earthly experience in the Incarnation; it is the source of all his thoughts and actions. Jesus came into the world for the Father and for his glory; the doctrine he preaches has been given him by the Father; the miracles he performs are the work of the Father; the Person he reveals is that of the Father.

"I live because of the Father." [1] These words disclose the secret of his life. The Father is the origin and the goal of his earthly existence. What precisely is meant by life "because of the Father"? The expression

[1] John 6:58.

has a double meaning: for the sake of the Father or out of regard for him, and by virtue of the Father. According to the first meaning Christ lives for the sake of the Father; he is completely devoted to his cause. According to the second meaning he lives by virtue of the life he has received from the Father. The latter meaning is more ontological and biological in the sense that the Father appears as the origin and source from which the life of Jesus continually derives its existence. The former meaning is more psychological: the Father is the goal Christ sets himself, the person for whose love he is willing to dedicate all his efforts. In the basic theology of the Gospel of St. John the psychological and the biological points of view are joined together. When Christ is presented as the life of Christians, it is always meant that he is a higher form of life which enters into the human soul and penetrates it with an entirely new disposition, that of love. Furthermore, this love is not presented merely as a psychological attitude; it is felt to be something real and vital, far greater than any conscious or actual manifestation of it. Life is thus raised to the level of love, and love takes on a deeper significance as life. This mutual penetration of the psychological and the ontological may be expressed by the equation: life-love.

This equation helps to clarify the meaning of the words of Jesus: "I live because of the Father." Christ lives because of the life which the Father communicates to him; this sharing of life also involves a sharing of love, which causes Jesus to live not only by means of the Father, but for him. To live because of the Father necessarily involves leading a human life, because the Father has so willed it, because the Father has sent his Son into this world. The biological existence of Christ and the beating of his human heart are the natural consequences of that love which causes him to acquiesce completely in the will of his Father. To live because of the Father means to realize perfectly that it is the Father who confers existence. It also means to have no other object in life than the Father, no other ideal than to accomplish his will. Jesus proceeds from the Father to the Father. He comes from him and he goes back to him. Through prayer he is again absorbed in that source from which his earthly existence is derived; through his teaching, his actions, and his sacrifice he aims at the glorification of the Father. This whole movement of the human existence of the Word is effectively presented by St. John as a kind of immobility; Jesus is in the Father, he remains in the Father. The love of the Father, which is expressed in the earthly activity of Jesus, is so deeply imbedded in his heart that it has the force of eternal life; its movement is a state of repose.

His fundamental humility

In his eagerness to glorify the Father Christ will not permit men's devotion to be focused upon himself. The rich young man who was suddenly struck by the goodness of Jesus and rushes up to humble himself

3

before him, saying "Good Master," is reminded that the glory of all goodness should be referred to the Father: "None is good, except God only." [2] Jesus does not wish the young man, who has obviously been carried away by a sudden feeling of enthusiasm, to attribute the divine goodness to himself alone; if he reveals himself to men as God, it is as the Son of the Father, of a Father from whom he has received all things. His reply seems to be marked by a certain amount of feeling, as if he had been taken back by what he heard and was anxious to relieve this feeling by setting matters straight. The devotion of this young man, which amounted to treating him as a new God in place of the old, affected him in a very sensitive spot, his complete devotion to the Father. The love of Jesus for the Father is such that he cannot endure even the slightest disparagement of the Father.

This is an excellent example of Christ's humility. We are wont to marvel at the humility he displayed towards his disciples and towards mankind in general, a humility symbolized by the washing of the feet. But this humility towards men is only the consequence of a deeper and more fundamental humility towards the Father. The most remarkable feature about this humility is that it belongs to a God who became man. If we had been free to imagine the manner of God's appearance on earth, we might have supposed, logically enough, that he would have chosen to reveal himself as the one, supreme Master, who would make

[2] Mark 10:18.

known his teaching to men and who would cause all religious worship and all devotion to be paid to himself. The wise in the philosophy of this world would not have failed to point out that God could hardly be expected to be humble if he came to live among men, because humility is a virtue which belongs to our status as creatures. It is a virtue which belongs to one who does not exist in his own right and who must receive everything from his Creator; it is the counterpart in the moral order of the basic dependence of creatures on God in the ontological order. If the Creator should enter this world, he could not share in this dependence of creatures and, consequently, could have no part in their humility. He alone would have the right not to be humble, and we might even say that he had the duty not to be, since truth required that he should conduct himself as the Supreme Being. Reasoning in this way we should have been inclined to exclude humility from the role of an incarnate God.

Now revelation presents us with an entirely different picture. The whole life of Christ, as God and Creator, is permeated with humility and rests upon humility to such an extent that St. Paul is able to sum up the work of redemption in the Incarnation as self-denial and obedience. The one we should have thought had a right to be completely self-centered dedicates himself to us in a spirit of complete disregard for self. He presents himself not as one who has come on his own initiative or as a result of the supreme decree of his own will, but as one who has been sent by another. He does not tell his apostles that the doctrine he offers them is one which he himself has worked out or conceived in the genius of his wisdom; he has received his teaching from another. From another likewise comes the impressive power which is revealed in the miracles he performs. Far from desiring to force himself on them because of his own person or origin, he appeals to the mandate he has received from another, in order to cause them to believe in him. Although he is God, or rather precisely because he is God, Christ is well aware that the self is an object of hatred and that this is more likely to be true in his own case than it would be in the case of creatures among whom he has come to live. His self therefore remains hidden behind another. The God who became man is more profoundly humble than men.

We have just said that he is humble because he is God.

As a matter of fact, the humility of Jesus is so basic that it appears in his divine status as the Son. Is it not obvious that the Word, begotten by the Father, is in the position of one who has received all from another? Is it not true that the eternal attitude of the Word consists in forgetting himself in order to glorify the Father, in contemplating the Father's greatness and goodness without end? From all eternity the Son rejoices in owing everything to the Father, in humbling himself in his own sight, so that he may fasten his gaze on the countenance of the Father. Jesus is

6

simply expressing this eternal attitude of the Word in his thoughts and acts as a man.

Humility inspired by love

Complete and absolute as his humility is, how natural and to a certain extent how easy Christ makes this attitude seem in his case. He delights in submission to the Father, he is completely at ease in his submission, and he would not change his attitude for anything else in the world. Why is this? Because his humility is wholly the result of love. When we love someone else sincerely, we are apt to forget ourselves in thinking of the other person; when we are filled with love, we cannot refrain from telling everybody what we think about the one who is loved. Christ is possessed and absorbed by his love for the Father; that is why he takes pleasure in speaking about him continually, in humbling himself before him, in recognizing that he has received everything from him, and in attributing to him full merit for the plan of redemption. He is glad to remain in the background of the glory he is able to win for the Father. Towards the close of his life he speaks to the Father in summing up the work of his mission here on earth: "I have exalted thy glory on earth." [3] He wishes the glory of his resurrection, which is destined to crown the work of redemption, to reflect glory on the Father: "Father, the time has come; give glory now to thy Son, that thy

[3] John 17:4.

7

Son may give glory to thee." [4] All glory must be finally attributed to the Father and to him alone.

We now begin to understand the true proportions of the humility of Jesus. It is not at all like a narrow mould which imprisons the soul in depressing thoughts. Jesus thinks only of the greatness of the Father, and far from shrinking at the thought his soul is filled with great enthusiasm. His humility is the sound of a great triumph echoing within him, the triumph of the Father, in whom he is content to lose himself.

There is no attempt on the part of Christ to parade his humility. It flows quite naturally from his love. Jesus humbles himself in the sight of the Father, because he is wholly taken up with him and continually prefers him to himself. He rejects the unnecessarily severe and unrealistic attitude of those who are inclined to deny the existence of good qualities which they actually possess. The humility of Jesus is unquestionably perfect, but in another sense: it is founded on the conviction that he has received everything from the Father. There is no exception to this "everything." Jesus is well aware that he owes absolutely everything to him. Instead of wishing to deny or to minimize the extent to which he owes everything to the Father, he is at pains to point out the value and excellence of what he owes to him. He does not hesitate to speak of himself as Master and Lord, to mention the beauty of the work he has performed, and to declare his own

[4] John 17:1.

8

glory. He proclaims that he is the light of humanity, the good shepherd who has come to gather in all his sheep, one gentle and humble of heart who brings comfort to all. He declares that he is the fountain of life and predicts that all men will be drawn towards him, for all this comes from the Father and is meant to redound to his honor.

Inspired by love this humility of Jesus is a remarkably dynamic force. It is constructive; it desires to build something on a vast and grandiose scale: the glory of the Father. For the sake of this glory Christ is prepared to submit to the lowest form of human degradation, shame, and misery. He is prepared for its sake to wear himself out in the course of his public ministry without counting the cost. As he goes the rounds of the villages of Galilee and Judea, walking for days on end without showing any signs of fatigue, he is carried along by the love of the Father. He is even prepared to go to the ends of the world, if this love had not confined him to the borders of Palestine. When he preaches for endless hours to the crowds who are destined to lose on the morrow the seed he has scattered among them today, love of the Father is what inspires his heart and sustains his voice. Sometimes, when he is teaching in the temple, he is so consumed by the fire of this love that he cries out. What is it that he cries? The name of him who fills his heart, the Father. Confronted by the unbelief of the Pharisees, Jesus makes a supreme effort to proclaim the

9

dearly beloved Father: "I have not come of my own impulse, I was sent by one who has a right to send; and him you do not know. I know him, because I come from him; it was he who sent me." [5] Again towards the close of his ministry he cries out, so St. John tells us, his last words to the crowd: "If a man believes in me, it is in him who sent me, not in me, that he believes. . . . Everything, then, which I utter, I utter as my Father has bidden me." [6]

Submission to the Father is thus what inspires him to develop the great range of his talents and to undertake his great work. The problem of reconciling his self-abasement and humility with the full development of his faculties and heart thus appears to be resolved in the case of Christ. The same problem confronts his followers today and demands a solution in Christian humanism. How can we reconcile the development of personality with the injunction which requires us to be humble and renounce self? If we argue from the standpoint of what is thought to be good for the human ego and insist upon separating the divine and human spheres, we are bound to reach the one-sided and unsatisfactory conclusion that selfishness appears to be justified and that there is little or no point in making any sacrifices. Christ shows that the real solution is to be found in love, in total love. It is not essential to know what the needs of the self are, but what those of love are; that is to say, the needs and the wishes of someone else. Christ is governed

[5] John 7:28–29.   [6] John 12: 44, 50.

throughout his life by the Father; he carries the kingdom of God within him before imparting it to the world. Instead of being formed of two separate parts, man and God, he is moved only by the will of the Father. It is the Father who unifies his existence, causes his heart to beat, and brings about the full development of his faculties. In the midst of self-abasement and humiliation this love of the Father continues to inspire his soul.

Submission unto the cross

Love makes the humility of Christ seem natural and his submission seem easy, but it could not exempt him from renunciation. Man is naturally inclined to think of love as consisting entirely of charm, and humility as consisting entirely of sweetness. But the submission of Jesus involved terrible losses, which he must have keenly felt. Can we imagine how difficult it must have been for a person of his stature to have to live for thirty years in the village of Nazareth? He was obliged throughout this time to conceal his great talents in the performance of some utterly trivial work, which anyone could have performed in his place. The one who had come into the world to save souls and knew that he was destined to bring about the salvation of mankind was obliged to content himself with planing wood, while on all sides his ears and his eyes were accosted by the distress of souls. How painful it must have been for him to have to close his heart to these appeals! Yet close it he must, so that his heart might remain open to the will of his Father. When his imprisonment in Nazareth came to an end, it was succeeded by another kind of imprisonment. The new prison was much larger, to be sure, but it was still a prison. Christ was obliged by the Father to spend the entire period of his ministry within the narrow boundaries of Palestine: "My errand is only to the lost sheep that are of the house of Israel." [7] Now there can be no doubt that he had great love for all mankind and longed to go to the help of all; this barrier imposed by the Father shattered dreams that were very dear to his heart and prevented him from realizing great hopes. Christ was a missionary at heart. He longed to appeal to the people of all nations, for he shared none of the narrow nationalist prejudices of his fellow-countrymen. How impatient he is to summon all souls to the kingdom of God! He repeats over and over again that the hour has now come when all people shall enter into this kingdom. Yet he is not permitted to bring them the good news himself. He has only a brief opportunity to do so in passing through the land of Tyre and Sidon. He is obliged to confine his ministry to Judea and Galilee, content on occasion to show his special regard for strangers by praising the Roman centurion or the Samaritan leper. One who might have embraced the whole world must have found the boundaries of Palestine exceedingly narrow! If the Father had so willed, Christ would have gladly undertaken to spread the Gospel over the whole

[7] Matt. 15:24.

world; he would have walked the paths that St. Paul was later to follow in weariness and gladness. But the Father does not will it, and Christ acquiesces in his decision with his whole heart, without showing any sign of regret or impatience.

Instead of sending him to spread the Gospel far and wide, the Father leads Jesus to the shame of Calvary. That is to be the consummation of his mission on earth. We see by his struggle during the passion that it must have been painful for him to have to accept this. Christ buried deep within his soul the traces of other sacrifices he was obliged to make, but the approach of the sacrifice of the cross affects him to such an extent that he is unable to conceal his despair. The struggle engages his whole being, and we must observe Christ at Gethsemani if we would realize the full extent of the torture which love of the Father is capable of inflicting on him, a love so terrible in what it requires of him, and so apparently cruel and brutal. In order to accept it completely, Jesus must submit to a sundering of his body and soul.

His agony continues on the cross. Christ is tortured by the thought of being abandoned by the Father, but he succeeds nevertheless in abandoning himself to him. Before drawing his last breath he cries out: "Father, into thy hands I commend my spirit." [8] This last appeal is the final outburst of his consuming love. Magnificent and moving as this act of abandonment is, can we imagine what this willing submission

[8] Luke 23:46.

13

on his part meant to Jesus? Surrendering his life to the Father means acquiescing in the termination of his life in the midst of his youth, after scarcely two years of public activity; it means resigning himself to seeing his human capabilities, which are so full of promise, condemned once and for all and the final ruin of the tremendous possibilities of his ministry. It means that he must allow himself to be torn from the loving companionship of his mother and his apostles and generally from the society of men whom he loved so deeply. Man feels the separation involved in death more or less keenly depending upon the strength of his affections. Christ is pained at the thought of having to leave men because he loved them so very dearly. In his final appeal to the Father the offering of his love clearly bears the mark of this intense grief.

Submission unto victory

Painful as this submission to the Father must have been in itself, Jesus was not spared the attacks of his enemies in this quarter. It is the foundation-stone of the work of redemption which Satan is at all costs anxious to uproot. We find him approaching Jesus who has been worn out by his fasting in the desert. What does he propose? He bids Jesus obtain bread for himself; at least that is what he appears to be doing on the surface. In reality however he is urging Jesus to employ his power as the Messias in an arbitrary and absolute way without regard for the purpose which the Father had in mind when he conferred this power on him. He is suggesting that he employ his miraculous power to satisfy a purely personal end without regard for the work of redemption and the salvation of souls; in other words, he would have him betray the Father. He endeavors to persuade Christ by employing the very title he would wrest from him: "If thou art the Son of God . . ." [9] The Son of God is Master, supreme and free to do as he wills. If Satan could only turn this Son of God against God himself! In order to accomplish this, he must first destroy the filial heart of Christ; but it is this very heart which resists all his efforts. Christ is nourished by the words which proceed from the mouth of God. Satan again attempts to undermine the submission of Jesus in another way; he proposes that the work of redemption should be facilitated by the performance of some spectacular miracle, by Christ's casting himself down from the pinnacle of the temple. His efforts are in vain, for he receives the reply: "Thou shalt not put the Lord thy God to the proof." [10] Christ, by remaining unshakable in his subservience to the Father, rejects the false notion that the Son of God might be willing to carry out the plan of redemption to please himself and in the easiest possible way. Finally, Satan offers him a compromise in the conquest of the world, if he will render unto the fallen angel the worship which should be paid to the Father. As in the case of the two previous temptations the immediate reaction of Jesus shows that he is completely and exclusively submissive to the will of the

[9] Matt. 4:3.   [10] Matt. 4:7.

15

Father. He is victorious in defending the possession which is dearest to his heart, his fundamental love for the Father.

Satan will renew his attacks in the course of Christ's public life. He will inspire the relatives of Jesus and the Pharisees to request the performance of miracles. He will attempt to divert Christ from the road to Calvary by the reproaches of Peter. All these attempts are destined to fail. Satan will make one last attempt to destroy this submission to the Father when Christ is beset by pangs of fear and a feeling of revulsion during his agony in the garden. Satan is lurking in the shadows of Gethsemani. Although driven by fear and sadness to ask that the cup be taken away, Jesus nevertheless remains absolutely firm in his resolve to comply with the wishes of the Father: "Only as thy will is, not as mine is." [11] Each wave of fear and despair causes Satan to hope that he is at last about to sever the bond of submission, but each time the bond holds true. In this awful struggle which tugs at the very heart-strings of Jesus the Father remains victorious.

Throughout the ministry of Jesus the Pharisees also constantly strive to discover, or they would force him to disclose to them, some basic weakness in this filial submission to the Father. They are always spying on Christ in order to discover him in some transgression of the divine will, no matter how slight. They are anxious to separate his cause from that of God and

[11] Mark 14:36.

take him to task for what they consider to be viola-
tions of the Sabbath. "This man can be no messenger
from God; he does not observe the sabbath. . . . This
man, to our knowledge, is a sinner." [12] They subject
his doctrine to the most careful kind of scrutiny in
order to discover some contradiction with the teachings which God has revealed to the Jewish people.
Their questions are full of pitfalls and are calculated
to catch him in some error for which they vainly look
in his sermons. Each one of their questions is turned
against them. "Can any of you convict me of sin?" [13]
he retorts. In spite of their tactics the Pharisees are
unable to discover the slightest crack in the submission of Christ to the Father. On the one occasion
when they are confident they have caught their oppo-
nent in the act of committing a blasphemy, in the case
of the lame man whose sins are forgiven, Jesus proves
that he is acting in complete accord with the Father
by performing a miraculous cure. They are unable to
allege any serious charge against him at his trial and
are unsuccessful in their attempt to separate his cause
from that of God. Only his enemies believe the taunt
hurled at him on the cross: "Rescue thyself; come
down from that cross, if thou art the Son of God." [14]
It is the same skeptical strain heard before in the
desert: "If thou art the Son of God." The words
sound like Satan's cry of rage as he finally realizes that
the game is lost and that he has failed to separate the

[12] John 9:16, 24.   [14] Matt. 27:40.
[13] John 8:46.

Son from the Father through fear of torture. They also betray the helplessness of the Pharisees who are unable to harm further the one whom they have crucified and who wish to persuade themselves that his cross is a mark of divine displeasure. The words of the centurion however vindicate Jesus by emphasizing his oneness with the Father: "No doubt but this was the Son of God." [15] Christ loved the Father so much and conformed himself so perfectly to his will, that even a stranger could recognize in his face and in his dying words the countenance and voice of Almighty God.

Son of God

Although his enemies never succeeded in robbing this storehouse of his filial heart, their hostility compelled him to keep it well hidden and to reveal its existence only with the greatest care. Jesus would proudly have borne the name of "Son of God," which is so expressive of all that he is, and would freely have spoken of his intimacy with the Father as he did among his apostles. But he was compelled to minimize this aspect; instead of calling himself the "Son of God," he designates himself by the more mysterious title of "Son of Man," a title which belongs to the Messias, but one which does not allow him to express the deepest feelings of his heart. He has to be extremely cautious in this whole matter. Because of the hostile feelings of the Pharisees which are rife among the crowd, he might run the risk of alienating his hearers rather than winning them over if he calls him-

[15] Mark 15:39.

self the Son of God too openly. The only one who shows no hesitation in attributing this title to him is his chief enemy, Satan. He employs it during the temptations in the desert; and the devils, whom Jesus casts out of possessed persons, frequently fling at him by way of revenge: "Thou art the Son of God." Just as Satan appealed to his nature as the Son of God when he wished to suggest an act of disobedience, so he malignantly casts in Christ's face the name of Son of God when he wishes to provoke an unfavorable reaction among the crowd. He endeavors to turn this name, which ought to serve as a rallying point for love, into a weapon of hate. Christ orders him to be silent and represses in his own heart the desire he has to proclaim the true meaning of this name far and wide. This desire must be continually suppressed until the moment when Caiphas puts the question to him he has been longing to answer, as a kind of final charge: "I adjure thee by the living God to tell us whether thou art the Christ, the Son of God?" [16] At last the heart of Christ is free to cast off the great burden: "Thy own lips have said it." "I am." [17] He is able at last to declare aloud before the religious leaders of the Jewish people what the essential bond is which unites him with his God and to guarantee this statement by the sacrifice of his life. The solemn adjuration of the high priest compels him to use this title and to declare with his own lips what he has always been, the Son of God.

[16] Matt. 26: 63.   [17] Matt. 26:64; Mark 14:62.

19

Encounters with the Father

The part played by memory tends to make Christ's love for his Father more powerful and dramatic. In order to explain human desire for the perfect good Plato developed the theory of a previous existence, according to which souls were believed to have once contemplated this good and then to have retained the memory of it during the shadows of their earthly existence. This previous existence, which has no real meaning as far as mankind is concerned, does reflect the situation of Christ, with the important difference that in his case it is not the past which enters the present, but eternity which enters time. Christ remembers the Father here on earth: "It was from the Father I came out, when I entered the world." [18] He occasionally refers to the state which preceded his appearance on earth: "Believe me, before ever Abraham came to be, I am." [19] He makes this statement in order to prove that he has knowledge of the Father: "You cannot recognize him. But I have knowledge of him." [20]

By means of the hypostatic union the human heart of Christ is joined to this eternal knowledge which the Word has of the Father. In order to understand his heart, we must go back to the Word. Hence St. John, who discloses many details about the intimate life and deepest thoughts of Jesus, begins his Gospel with an account of the Word: "In the begin-

---

[18] John 16:28.   [20] John 8:54–55.
[19] John 8:58.

ning was the Word, and the Word was with God."
The Son is turned towards the Father in the most
complete kind of union. From all eternity he is not
attached to himself but adheres to the Father in an
infinite love and in an inseparable embrace. If the
earthly eyes of Christ are lifted towards the Father, it
is because the love of the Word is already turned in
this direction.

The whole power of eternal love presses at the
door of the human heart of Jesus. The presence of this
divine intimacy is what directs all the thoughts of
Christ towards the Father; he is turned towards him
eagerly and breathlessly. We are now in a position to
appreciate why Christ, who was obliged to hide the
splendor of his divinity during his life as a man, is so
fond of finding himself in the presence of his Father.
Does he not abandon his parents at the age of twelve
in order to remain in his Father's house, the temple?
The walls of the temple are cold and bare and scarcely
evoke his recollection of the eternal dwelling-place;
the temple is also encumbered with merchants and
money-changers; there is a surfeit of sacrifices and
not nearly enough love. But where merchants are
thinking of profits and the priests about ritual matters
Jesus is filled with joy, because he is aware of the divine presence. The rest hardly counts. His Father is
there; with him there is complete contentment. When
he enters the building he finds himself, as it were,
again in heaven. He lifts his face and his heart to the
Father and lets them share in that devotion which has

existed from all eternity. In allowing his eyes to be filled with the sight of the Father, he feels that he is himself once more: "Could you not tell that I must needs be in the place that belongs to my Father?" [21]

Later on during his public ministry Christ frequently withdraws from the others in order to pray in silence. Before embarking upon his ministry he thus withdraws into the desert. During the course of his preaching, when the evening finally comes after a day filled with fatigue, he is pictured as withdrawing in silence. What a silence this must have been! The solitude his heart knows so well, the solitude he has always shared with another and which the Word had "in the beginning" with the Father. It is from this unchanging intimacy that Jesus derives the strength he needs to carry on to the end of his human existence. He offers all to the Father and receives all from him. His whole earthly life with its burden of sorrow and trouble, struggle and effort, is passed in the continual give and take of their intimacy.

The Gospel sheds no light on what was actually said during these hours of prayer. Intimate conversations of this sort are generally not recorded for publication. But the Gospel describes various other occasions when Jesus was enthusiastic about encountering the Father in things and in men. While he loves to commune with the Father in solitude, Jesus equally marvels at the traces of the Father's presence wherever he goes. Everything speaks to him of the

[21] Luke 2:49.

22

Father's greatness and goodness. Even the humblest creatures embody the immenseness of the divine love. In small, ordinary flowers, such as the lilies of the field which are thoughtlessly plucked and cast away, Jesus recognizes the loving care of the Father who has conferred on them a garment finer than Solomon's. In the same way the little birds appear to be the object of the Father's constant and tender care, for he nourishes them although they neither sow nor reap. For Christ the world is not composed primarily of things which are destined to serve the needs of man, or of the marvelous order of the laws of nature, or of matter in relation to spirit, or of poetic harmony which is meant to appeal to the eye; it is above all the living language of the Father, the manifestation of his goodness. Jesus knows the Father so well and looks only for him; he finds his presence in every detail of the universe and derives an immense satisfaction from the discovery.

He derives an even greater satisfaction when he encounters the Father in men. While Jesus teaches his disciples not to despise the flowers and the birds, he enjoins them above all to be careful about despising the small and the weak among men. "See to it that you do not treat one of these little ones with contempt; I tell you that they have angels of their own in heaven, that behold the face of my heavenly Father continually." [22] That is to say, the face of the Father which the angels behold is reflected in their faces and makes them holy. If Jesus teaches his disciples to rec-

[22] Matt. 18:10.

23

ognize the Father's face in the poor and in the unfortunate, is it not because he himself is aware of the presence of God in these unfortunate creatures, in the same way that we are able to recognize the features of a parent in any human face, and because he treats them with the respect and tenderness the divine face calls for?

But Jesus is above all fond of discovering the Father in souls. The examples of faith he calls forth on all sides are the fruit of the Father's work, and the attraction which he himself has for human hearts is recognized as the result of invisible action on the part of the Father. "Nobody can come to me without being attracted towards me by the Father who sent me." [23] On the road to Caesarea, when Peter is asked what he thinks of the person of Jesus and declares his faith in the words: "Thou art the Christ," the Master at once points out the enlightening presence of God in this answer. It is as if the Father had just spoken to him through the mouth of the apostle. "Blessed art thou, Simon son of Jona; it is not flesh and blood, it is my Father in heaven that has revealed this to thee." [24] Jesus is delighted when he sees little children coming towards him who are not remarkable either for their intelligence or their learning, because the simplicity of their souls emphasizes the splendor of the faith that has been given them and makes the divine origin of this faith all the more apparent. He sees in this a further manifestation of the Father's marvelous work

[23] John 6:44.　　　　　　　[24] Matt. 16:17.

and is greatly pleased. "At this time, Jesus was filled with gladness by the Holy Spirit, and said, O Father, who art Lord of heaven and earth, I give thee praise that thou hast hidden all this from the wise and the prudent, and revealed it to little children. Be it so, Lord, since this finds favor in thy sight." [25] The Evangelist mentions that this gladness is felt by Jesus "in the Holy Spirit." As the love which unites the Son with the Father, the Holy Spirit causes the heart of Christ to overflow, when it encounters the goodness of the Father. Before crying from the depths of Christian souls: "Abba, Father," [26] the Spirit lets this cry rise from the heart of Jesus himself.

Christ not only expresses his enthusiasm; he explains the profound reasons for it: "None knows the Son truly except the Father, and none knows the Father truly except the Son, and those to whom it is the Son's good pleasure to reveal him." [27] For one to be able to recognize the Son of God in the man Jesus, the Father must exist, the Father who knows the Son from all eternity. It is the Father who inspires acts of faith in Christ. For one to be able to recognize the Father in the creatures of this world and especially in the actions of believers, the Son who knows the Father from all eternity must exist. By virtue of his eternal knowledge of the Father, Jesus is able to recognize him in the little children who come before him; this is the spark which touches off his hymn of thanksgiving. The recognition of his mind transforms itself im-

[25] Luke 10:21.   [27] Matt. 11:27.
[26] Gal. 4:6.

mediately into an effective expression of his gratitude. We grasp the full meaning of this gratitude in the case of Jesus only if we see it as the expression of an eternal vision which pierces the darkness of earthly things.

Abandonment and unity

The keenness with which Christ perceived the presence of the Father in nature and in men helps to explain the real suffering he experienced when he was abandoned by the Father during his passion. The one who shook with joy whenever he encountered the unforgettable presence of the Father during the course of his life was obviously saddened to the point of death when the Father ceased in any perceptible way to signify his love and pleasure to him during the passion. While he was being tortured on the cross, this absence of the divine presence caused him to let out a cry of indescribable anguish: "My God, my God, why hast thou forsaken me?" [28] He whose heart had always been filled with the Father, who borrowed from him the substance of his thoughts, the strength with which he moved, and the inspiration for his emotions and feelings, suddenly found himself cut off from this dearly-beloved Father in the midst of the cruelest of all trials. It was as if the inner world of Jesus were crumbling, as if he were losing the support on which he had depended throughout his whole life, as if a chasm had suddenly yawned where before there had always been countless riches. Abandonment by the Father was the

[28] Matt. 27:46.

great suffering Christ had to bear, incomparably more terrible and agonizing than all the other trials to which he had to submit. This indeed marked the hour of darkness.

Yet throughout this period of heart-rending agony his essential unity with the Father remains intact. The words which Jesus pronounced on an earlier occasion are still valid: "He who sent me is with me; he has not left me alone, since what I do is always what pleases him." [29] "Do you not believe that I am in the Father, and the Father is in me? The words I speak to you are not spoken of my own impulse; and the Father, who dwells continually in me, achieves in me his own acts of power." [30] Can the cross, the very work of the Father, be displeasing to the Father; and is the Father not present in him who is crucified? Christ himself warns his disciples: "Behold, the time is coming, nay, has already come, when you are to be scattered, each of you taking his own path, and to leave me alone. And yet I am not alone, because the Father is with me." [31] When the hour of final tribulation arrives, the Father remains in Christ more firmly than ever before and the moment of awful abandonment becomes at the same time the moment of complete union.

Here we touch upon the most profound mystery of the heart of Christ. Looking at things from the human point of view, we should never have thought that Christ could feel abandoned by the Father, and

[29] John 8:29.
[30] John 14:10.
[31] John 16:32.

27

what is even more mystifying, that this moment of separation should be accompanied by the closest kind of unity. Christ shows us, however, that the cruel suffering occasioned by his abandonment, which would normally involve a cessation and failure of love, as a matter of fact tends to serve as a vigorous kind of stimulus towards more love. He thus shows how, in so many mystical experiences, the soul experiences distress by the absence of God at the very moment when it is exceedingly near to him, and this feeling of abandonment serves notably to increase the soul's fervor. The darkness of Golgotha is repeated during those nights when souls devoted to God seem to call upon him in vain; the Lord conceals himself in them on such occasions, in order to penetrate them more completely; he escapes from their view, in order to attach them to himself more closely, in order to take full possession of them. Jesus above all demonstrates how Christians are expected to endure trials by showing us that suffering can serve greatly to strengthen love. When love appears to be the most agonizing and the most agonized, it can become the most ardent and the most unifying. When man suffers, he is conscious of loving more sincerely. If he is torn from the person he loves and accepts this separation generously, he finds that his love for the person tends to increase and his sense of union takes on a deeper meaning. He feels lifted by his sacrifice to a higher kind of intimacy. We see from the example of Christ that suffering of this sort was not foreign to the purest and noblest kind of love which ever moved a human heart, his love for the Father.

The example of Jesus also shows that the beneficial effect of suffering is not limited to its role in purifying the human ego. It does wipe out sin and possesses an expiatory and redemptive value. But we can see from the life of Christ that it is not merely a kind of purification which precedes love; Jesus had no need of purification in his innocent state. Suffering is the fruit of love, a fruit which brings about an increase in love and causes love to develop to the fullest extent. Faced by the absolute void of his abandonment Jesus cries for help; can there be any outburst more heartfelt than his prayer at Gethsemani, when he clings to the Father with all the strength his burdened soul is capable of? From the cross he cries to the Father: "Eloi . . ." These words seem to be torn from his tortured breast; they express the unbelievable fervor of his love, the more consuming the more it is tortured. Suffering is thus capable of producing love; the most original and most compelling example of this is to be found in the human heart of Christ, which was torn from the Father and united with him again.

Gift of the Father

The Father is the one on whom Jesus ultimately relies throughout his earthly life, but he does not keep him to himself. The Word assumed a human heart for the purpose of communicating the one he loves to mankind; Jesus shares the Father with us. The kingdom of God which he has come to found on earth consists in a general extension of the fatherhood of the Father. Jesus never tires of speaking about the Father to his disciples and causes them to admire him, because he sincerely wants to give him to them.

He teaches his apostles the way in which they should henceforth pray to God: "Our Father, who art in heaven . . ." Only Christ had the power to authorize men to address God in this fashion. The use of these words with reference to God amounts to a revolution. The Old Testament was no doubt familiar with the idea of God's paternal goodness, but no one would have dared to use the words "Our Father" in praying to God, who was thought of as a transcendent and majestic Being. Man's initial impulse, when he prostrated himself before the divinity, was to sink down in adoration before him; it would have seemed presumptuous to call upon him directly as Father. Man strove to gain the divine favor by humbling himself completely before God's supreme power. Christ causes the supreme power of God to appear in a new light, as the authority of a Father. If a man wishes to obtain his favor, he must henceforth appeal to God's fatherly love.

In sharing the Father with us Jesus is anxious to have us share in his filial heart. The words of this prayer, which he gave us, are meant to inculcate a twofold attitude with regard to the heavenly Father. The first and basic attitude consists in desiring the glorification of God's name, the coming of his kingdom, and the doing of his will. The lips of Jesus tremble with joy as they impress this threefold desire on the memory of his apostles, a desire which dominated his whole life and is destined to become the prayer of countless generations. This request sums up the supreme desire of his heart. The hardest struggles in his life, his temptation in the desert and his passion, are destined to be fought over this issue; it is the Father's will which triumphs over all obstacles.

Having stressed the necessity of this fundamental attitude, Jesus desires to impress upon his disciples that they must be prepared to entrust themselves wholeheartedly and abandon all their cares to the heavenly Father. He therefore urges them to ask for their daily bread. He knows only too well that man is not readily inclined to believe in the divine goodness; he is prone to distrust a God of vengeance and to rebel against a harsh and cruel God. He even entertains the perverse notion that he may receive evils and chastisement from God in return for requests for certain earthly goods. Examples of this distrust in the divine goodness occur even among the very followers of Jesus. He deals with these on each occasion by asserting in categorical fashion the goodness of the heavenly Father; the sharpness of his reply indicates that he must have been deeply hurt by the implication. Are we prepared to believe that God would allow himself to be inspired by despicable motives which we would hesitate to attribute even to the most wretched of human fathers? "If any one of yourselves is asked by his son for bread, will he give him a stone? If he is asked for a fish, will he give him a serpent instead? Why, then, if you, evil as you are, know well enough how to give your children what is good for them, is not your Father in heaven much more ready to give wholesome gifts to those who ask him?" [32] To enable men to understand the Father's goodness, which he himself contemplates in all its splendor, but which is hardly perceived by men at all, Christ employs many comparisons. If a man is willing to go out of his way to satisfy a solicitous friend, if a faithless and unscrupulous judge yields to the repeated entreaties of a poor widow, how much more likely will God be moved by our prayers? Since all these parables are far too weak to convey the meaning of such a sublime truth, Christ offers men a perfect image of the goodness of the Father in his own goodness. Indeed, his Incarnation has for its aim to make known to men this fundamental truth: the love of the Father for men. Jesus urges his apostles to pray for whatever they need, because prayer connotes confidence in this love.

Moreover, their confidence must be boundless as his own confidence is boundless. In allowing men to participate in his filial love he grants them a privilege we might have thought he would reserve for himself. Jesus knew that his prayers would be heard: "For myself, I know that thou hearest me at all times," [33] he tells the Father, when Lazarus is raised from the dead. He urges us; nay, he bids us to repeat these words for

[32] Matt. 7:9–11.   [33] John 11:42.

our sakes; he shares with us the certainty that our prayers will be heard: "Ask, and you shall receive. . . ." He will not allow us to have any further doubts about the goodness of the Father.

He also explains this goodness through his example. Jesus wishes us to reflect the Father just as he reflected him: "But you are to be perfect, as your heavenly Father is perfect." [34] The context shows that he has the divine goodness in mind: "Love your enemies . . . that so you may be true sons of your Father in heaven, who makes his sun shine on the evil and equally on the good, his rain fall on the just and equally on the unjust." [35] According to these words of Jesus the perfection of the Father consists in his universal love, which even embraces those who have offended him. Men ought to imitate him by loving their enemies. During his earthly life Christ is constantly endeavoring to discover the Father's image in nature and in men; his desire is to find the perfect image of the Father in those who pardon their enemies and love them. When he succeeds in causing the face of the Father and his infinite goodness to be reflected in human faces, he is well content with the success of his work.

In thus imparting the Father and his love to us, Jesus gives us the very substance of his heart. The goal of his earthly existence is to make his Father our Father; Christian salvation and perfection, the final reward of redemption, are comprised in sonship with

[34] Matt. 5:48.   [35] Matt. 5:44–46.

respect to the Father. While he, from the cross, gives us the great gift of himself and of his own mother, it is above all the heavenly Father whom he is giving us. The moment he quits this world, his Father becomes our Father. Hence he tells Mary Magdalen, after he has arisen: "Return to my brethren, and tell them this; I am going up to him who is my Father and your Father." [36] He calls his apostles brethren, thus signifying that they are the sons of the heavenly Father; he explicitly says "my Father and your Father." The first words addressed to the apostles after his resurrection assure them that God is their Father.

The one whom the Word contemplated from all eternity was "his" Father; the one whom Jesus joins again for all eternity after his resurrection and ascension into heaven is his Father and our Father. He ascends to him in order to prepare a place for his apostles, in order to speak to him about them, in order to win for them his Father's blessing. He treats with him henceforth as he would with our Father. In his intimate life with the Father, the closest and most absorbing kind of intimacy which has ever existed, men have now found a place. Jesus has introduced them into his eternal conversation with the Father and caused them to share in the eternal exchange of love between Father and Son. He has taken them deeply to his heart, which is above all turned towards the Father.

[36] John 20:17.

34

2. HEART FOND OF HIS MOTHER

The silence of Jesus

The affection Jesus has for Mary is quite different from his love for the Father. In teaching his disciples and in disputes with his enemies Christ never tires of proclaiming the bonds which unite him with the Father and of attributing to him all glory for his work as the Messias; but he consistently relegates the person of his mother to the background. Not once, in the words which have come down to us in the Gospels, does he have any direct words of praise for her. He recognizes that he has received all things from the Father and shows an exemplary filial attitude in this respect, but he is silent when it comes to recognizing any benefits which his filial heart has received from Mary or anything which he owes to her care. He is, of course, fully aware of the great debt he owes his mother, but in spite of the affection and gratitude he displays on numerous occasions he never says a word about it. His disciples are doubtless generally conscious of the greatness of Mary's position and have a certain regard for her, but they do not show her any of the reverence to which she is entitled. Only one person could have thrown light on this greatness; Jesus knew of the unique privilege of her Immaculate Conception and during those long years in Nazareth had ample opportunity to discover the rare beauty of his mother's soul. He alone could have told them about the inexhaustible goodness of her heart, her lofty purpose, her great love of God, and the splendor of her destiny, but he did not choose to do so. Not a word is devoted to the exaltation of Mary, whom the Church will so exalt in succeeding generations. He adopts a fixed policy of silence with regard to her; no other explanation is possible, for an attitude so consistently maintained cannot be attributed to mere chance. Jesus simply does not wish to speak about his mother.

Are we to interpret this as an indication that he had little affection for his mother? By no means. If the love of Christ for the Father is perfect, the love he has for his mother must share the same perfection. Would it be possible for one whose whole life is summed up in love and whose love for mankind is so conspicuous to have been indifferent to his mother? As a general rule men have the strongest and most enduring kind of affection for their mothers. Christ loved Mary with all the love of which his heart was capable, both as a child and as a man, but this love differs from his love for the Father. He loves Mary in silence and is anxious to avoid any public manifestation of this love for fear of spoiling it, or possibly losing it altogether; he desires to preserve the essential privacy of his love for his mother. The normal relations of mother and son suffice to explain this silence. Most men love their mothers so deeply that it would seem presumptuous to try to express their feelings in words, much less to exhibit them to public view. They know their mothers are greatly to be admired, but they do not seek to impose their attitude on others. It would be difficult in any case to describe a feeling of this sort in words, because it is based upon a great many personal contacts which cannot be communicated to others.

Christ would have found that the disciples could not have understood in any case, because the revelation of Mary's greatness would have been premature. Their minds were not yet ready to receive such a great truth. They must first understand the greatness of Jesus himself and the mystery of his divinity, before they could appreciate the exceptional beauty of Mary. It would have pleased Christ to call the Blessed Virgin "Mother of God," but how could he presume to refer to her in this way when he was forced to be so discreet in revealing his own divine nature as the "Son of God," and was obliged to use the more common designation "Son of Man"? Only his heart would know the boundless affection he had for his mother.

But the attitude of Jesus may also be justified in another way. His silence was in accordance with the express wishes of Mary herself. The Blessed Virgin would not have been pleased if her Son had spoken in

37

her praise, and public recognition would have embarrassed her. She always sought to remain in the background. We may say that she showed a certain feminine instinct which warned her against the dangers of assuming a public rôle. She felt that her life ought to be devoted to the loving care of members of her family and to providing them with a home where they could grow up in an atmosphere of simplicity and contentment. During the public life of her Son, Mary would endeavor to prolong the atmosphere of Nazareth by coming to his side from time to time. The most conspicuous example of this devotion was her presence at the foot of his cross. In order to play this rôle successfully, she was obliged to remain in the background as a private person. By remaining there she succeeded in being his mother to the very end.

The Holy Spirit added to her natural instincts as a woman and mother something suggested by his grace. He inspired the heart of Mary with a profound desire, in complete accord with her maternal love, to minimize her own importance in the sight of her Son. The purpose of this inspiration was to ensure that Jesus would not be overwhelmed by his mother's love while he was growing up. When it came time for him to assume the duties connected with his public ministry, Mary showed that she understood better than most women how important this attitude was. She knew that Jesus had the highest mission to perform as the Messias and that all his aspirations were directed towards the fulfilment of this mission. She desired nothing more than to be able to contribute to the success of this mission by humbling herself and honoring her Son. She only asked that she be allowed to remain in the obscurity to which she was attached and which befitted her status as a poor woman.

This fundamental wish of his mother was scrupulously respected by Jesus. He had no desire to disrupt her humble existence. Since she preferred silence, he was content to have it so and made no mention of her greatness. The Holy Spirit was the one who inspired Mary with this preference for silence, but he was also the one who inspired her lips to utter that magnificent hymn of praise, and who would eventually cause the true proportions of her soul to emerge from the darkness. Very little was said about her in the Gospels, but the Holy Spirit had his revenge, so to speak, in succeeding generations, by orienting the mind of the Church towards a fuller appreciation of Mary's rôle and towards a greater exaltation of her person. Christ turned over to the Holy Spirit the charge of proclaiming the honor and glory of his mother.

It is true, however, that Christ began this work himself by hinting at her greatness in various ways. By performing his first miracle at the request of his mother he emphasized the fact that she was the one who induced him to anticipate the occasion on which he was destined to reveal his power as the Messias, and by giving her to John during his last moments on the cross he indicated that she was to become the mother of mankind.

His apparent rudeness

Various passages in the Gospels suggest that he was inclined to treat his mother with a certain amount of rudeness. We may even say that he attempted to teach her a lesson on a number of occasions. When he wandered from the custody of his parents at the age of twelve and was found by them in the temple he answers her rather sharply: "What reason had you to search for me? Could you not tell that I must needs be in the place that belongs to my Father?" [1] Is he not suggesting here that it was wrong for his mother to search for him? Again at Cana, when Mary suggested that he perform a miracle, his answer seems to be equally abrupt: "Nay, woman, why dost thou trouble me with that? My time has not come yet." [2] Is it not possible to detect a certain amount of irritation in his words? Later, when Mary and his cousins came to see him and word was brought to him of their arrival, his answer seems to be even more unfriendly. Instead of being glad at the news and hastening to greet his family, his mother above all, he prefers to remain in the midst of the crowd with his newly found family. "Who is a mother, who are brethren, to me?" Looking at those who are seated around him in a circle, he says: "Here are my mother and my brethren! If anyone does the will of God, he is my brother, and

[1] Luke 2:49. [2] John 2:4.

sister, and mother." [3] He appears to consider his mother on a level with the other women in the crowd and to refuse her the special attention to which she has a right. Finally, when a woman of the people desires to praise his mother publicly: "Blessed is the womb that bore thee, the breast which thou hast sucked!" he turns this praise aside with the remark: "Shall we not say, Blessed are those who hear the word of God, and keep it?" [4] It could be maintained on the basis of these passages that Christ refuses to show any special regard for his mother, either by a display of affection, or by acquiescing in her praise, or by granting favors which she requests, and that whenever she attempts to intervene in the affairs of his public life, he rejects this intervention.

He thus not only appears to teach her a lesson on a number of occasions and assumes an attitude towards her bordering on cold indifference, but he even causes her pain. He might have spared her the anguish which she undoubtedly felt when he remained behind in the temple, but instead of apologizing for his action he justifies his conduct in a puzzling sort of way. Could he not have accomplished the will of the Father without offending his mother? His answer seems to indicate that he is oblivious of her anguish. Some have even maintained that Jesus could have prevented his mother from witnessing the horror of the crucifixion; he could have spared her the suffering caused by that terrible scene.

[3] Mark 3:33–35.   [4] Luke 11:27–28.

These objections are all based upon a reading of the Gospels which suggests that Jesus was not fully devoted to his mother. Such an interpretation is far too one-sided and betrays a failure to understand the true meaning of Christ's words.

We may say categorically that Christ was never rude to his mother, never wished to teach her a lesson, and did not wish to cause her any distress, except that which was inherent in her rôle as the mother of the Redeemer.

What reason had you to search for me?

When Jesus escapes from the custody of his mother at the age of twelve in order to be in the place belonging to his Father and thereby causes her anguish, he wishes to prepare Mary for the great test of Calvary, when he will be torn from her love to go to the Father, to be given back to her only after three days, when he has risen from the grave. This small incident foreshadows the drama of his death. Jesus is not unmindful of the distress he is causing his mother, any more than he will be unmindful of it when he is nailed to the cross and sees her in agony at his side. He knows that by causing her to suffer in this way he is only establishing her in her rôle as a participant in the work of redemption. He has confidence that Mary will have courage enough to assume this rôle without wavering; by causing her anguish in this way he assures himself that she will have the necessary strength of character to assume the burden of her rôle. In tearing the heart of his mother he is really tearing his own heart, but he must do so if the will of the heavenly Father is to be fulfilled. He makes it clear to Mary that he has wandered from her, not by accident or capriciously, but with a well-defined purpose in view: to be with the Father. He wishes to afford her some insight into the meaning of the mystery which she has already shared in her heart. At the time Mary did not understand the meaning of his words, but she kept them in her mind, endeavoring to penetrate the mystery and waiting for events to reveal the true meaning of what had happened. The incident does not tend to alienate his mother; it is used by Jesus as an occasion for associating her more closely with his future work of redemption by allowing her a glimpse of his divine Sonship and his relations with the Father. He introduces his mother to a higher level of maternal devotion and prepares her for his sacrifice. His love for Mary does not cause him to spare her from suffering; he wishes her heart to be able to bear the suffering which the Father has destined for him. The Father himself had already planted a sword of sorrow in her heart in the prophecy of Simeon; Jesus revives and enlarges this wound expressly for the purpose of preparing her for the part she is to play in his coming passion. His disappearance in the temple is not an attempt to separate himself from her, but an act by which he hopes to unite her with himself more closely than ever.

His reply must not be interpreted as an attempt

to teach Mary a lesson in the sense that he is rebuking her. Her reaction on this occasion is perfectly normal, because it is her duty as a mother to look for a son who has been lost. It is perfectly logical for her to ask for an explanation of his conduct, once he has been found. We should note carefully that Mary is not condemning Jesus for what he has done; she knows him too well not to guess that there is probably a hidden reason for his action. She simply asks a question, which perhaps betrays a certain amount of impatience because of the effort in finding him: "My Son, why hast thou treated us so?" There is nothing out of the ordinary in her behavior; everything is explicable in terms of her rôle as his mother. Jesus therefore is not blaming her for anything and could not blame her for anything. He answers her question by asking another himself: "What reason had you to search for me? Could you not tell that I must needs be in the place that belongs to my Father?" [5] This question sheds some light on the mystery. It is meant to arouse her curiosity by way of enlightening her, not by rebuking her. Far from desiring to expose the ignorance of his mother on this occasion, Jesus wishes to raise her to a higher level of understanding. The soul of Mary is not something which assumed its final form when it was fashioned by the Holy Spirit at the moment of her conception; it must develop, like all other human souls, and penetrate more deeply into the profound mystery surrounding her divine Son, gradually acquir-

[5] Luke 2:48, 49.

44

ing a more precise understanding of her rôle as his mother which will lead her to Calvary. Both her intelligence and her love must develop in accordance with the divine plan. The incident in the temple is used by Jesus as a means of furthering this development.

Why dost thou trouble me with that?

The marriage feast at Cana marks another step in this development. The reply of Jesus to his mother on this occasion must be understood with reference to the whole incident. His use of the word "woman" does not imply any indifference or rudeness on his part, for he employs the same term when he expresses his filial devotion so superbly on the cross, when he entrusts his mother to John: "Woman, this is thy son." [6] The term is simply used as an expression of good will. But the words: "Why dost thou trouble me with that," [7] appear to indicate a much stronger feeling. It has been correctly noted that the real attitude of Jesus when he spoke these words depends upon the way they were pronounced. The Gospel gives us the words, but says nothing about his attitude. Père Lagrange has noted with regard to a similar Arabic expression: "The real meaning of the word must be gathered from the way it is pronounced." We do not have any direct evidence with regard to the accent or tone Jesus used in his reply, but we may gather what his state of mind was from the context.

Jesus has just begun his public ministry and this

[6] John 19:26.　　　　　[7] John 2:4.

45

has brought about a change in his normal relations with his mother. Henceforth he no longer forms part of a household in which he is at the beck and call of his mother. He is now living independently and devoting himself to furthering his work as the Messias. Mary appears to be intervening in this work at Cana, when she pleads with her Son to perform a miracle. Her intervention seems to upset the divine plan. The occasion for his first miracle, an important act which is destined to reveal to the apostles and to others his power as the Messias and incline them to believe in him, has been determined by the Father. So it appears logical to believe that this interference by Mary in his public work is unseasonable. This perfectly natural objection is stated by Christ himself in the words: "Why dost thou trouble me with that, woman? My time has not yet come." Are his words meant as a refusal to do anything about the situation which his mother has called to his attention? He will later reply to the appeal of the Chanaanite woman by using a phrase which appears to be even more scathing, yet he agrees to grant her a miracle and only desires to test her faith. In this case he is testing the faith of his mother. Mary herself is not deceived by the meaning of the words she hears; she immediately understands that he is refusing her only for the sake of appearance. That is why she turns to the servants, no doubt with a reassuring smile, and says: "Do whatever he tells you." [8] She recognizes from the tone of her Son's reply

[8] John 2:5.

that he is ready to follow her suggestion and has only assumed this attitude for the purpose of graciously giving in to his mother's request. Her mother's intuition is immediately proved to be correct when he performs the miracle.

Instead of establishing a barrier between himself and Mary by adhering to his original objection, Christ wishes to show that he and his mother are of one mind by raising an objection which he immediately overcomes. He desires to make it clear that he is aware of the problem raised by the request of his mother and that it constitutes an interference in the work of his mission. If he had not spoken as he did, we might have thought that he was merely granting her a special request as an exception to a general rule, and that he had no intention of altering this rule; but since he acknowledges the right of his mother to intercede with him and influence the course of his public life, it is this right which he clearly recognizes when he performs the miracle. Although Mary only asked for a special favor, he replies by acknowledging her right to ask for favors and thus extends her rôle as mother to his whole work as the Messias. He will sanction this development of her rôle once and for all when he makes her the mother of mankind. At Cana, at the very beginning of his ministry, we find that he has already sanctioned this rôle as mother and mediatrix by performing at her request a miracle which clearly establishes his power as the Messias and causes the apostles to believe in him, thus inaugurating the reve-

47

lation of the divine message. In this way he makes Mary realize the importance of her power as his mother and the great significance of her mission.

Far from humiliating his mother on this occasion, he raises her to a fuller appreciation of her high rôle. Far from refusing her request, he opens the door of his heart to her more generously than ever before by associating her with the work of his ministry. But since he knows that Mary has no liking for public recognition of any kind, he is determined to proceed in a way that will not shock her sensibilities and will preserve her essential humility. His words are immediately understood by Mary. They were probably not very intelligible to those who happened to hear them and they would be baffling to the reader today if they were not accompanied by the gesture of the miracle which gives them their true meaning. Under an appearance of rudeness we can discern in these words the tender feelings of a truly filial heart which does honor to its mother, acknowledges her power, and crowns her efforts with success without outraging her simple, modest, and retiring way of life.

Here is my mother and here are my brethren

When his mother and cousins come to see him and Jesus tells the multitude that those who do the will of God are his brother, sister, and mother, he is not attempting to deprive his mother of her rightful place in his affection. He wishes to show that the duties of his ministry come before family obligations

48

and that his public life has given him a new family.
He is announcing in effect that the true bonds of affection are those which are founded on the desire to do
the will of God. This answer is especially directed at
his cousins. According to St. Mark they were endeavoring to persuade him to give up his public ministry
and return to his peaceful pursuits at Nazareth. They
did not believe in him or in his rôle as the Messias
and concluded that he must be mad. Before agreeing
to any discussion with them Christ wanted to make it
perfectly clear by what he said to the crowd that their
efforts to persuade him would be in vain. Henceforth
he belongs to a different family and no one can tear
him away from his work. He proves this by going on
with his sermon. His reply is also intended to make it
clear to his cousins that they can only resume their ties
of intimacy with him if they submit to the will of
God, a will that will cause them to have faith in him.
By his simple gesture in pointing to the crowd he contrasts their submissiveness to the will of God with the
unbelief of his cousins and indicates that the example
of the crowd is the one to follow. But this rebuke to
his cousins also implies an approval of Mary's action
on this occasion. She accompanies her relatives when
they come to see Jesus, but her purpose is quite different. The Blessed Virgin could never agree with them
that her Son had lost his mind or conspire with them
to bring him back home. She accompanies them for
the purpose of dissuading them from their intention
and protecting Jesus against their schemes. She hastens

to the side of her Son at a time when he is being threatened, as she will do when he is jeered at and abandoned by all. Her instinct as his mother is to join him, whenever a crisis develops in his life. It may be that the cousins hoped to derive from the presence of Mary some advantage in helping them to persuade Christ to give up his work, for word is brought that his mother is also there, with them. Jesus sees through this scheme by replying that every woman who does the will of God is his mother. This answer cannot have failed to please Mary, for she had hoped all along that his reply would be firm. Secretly, and in a language only comprehensible to their two hearts, Jesus is paying his mother a compliment. Is she not the woman who has best fulfilled the will of God? Has she not come to see that nothing shall interfere with the divine will and that his work as the Messias shall go on? Mary is thus his mother in a twofold sense: she brought him into the world and raised him, and on this occasion she shows that the important consideration with her is that the divine will be done.

Jesus wished to remind his cousins of the example of those who heard the will of God and believed in him. Did he also have to remind his mother of this? She was the first to hear his word and believe in him. She proved that she had faith in him at Cana by her confidence that he would supply the need for more wine before he had actually performed any miracle, and thus anticipated the acts of faith to be made by the apostles and others.

By refusing to listen to his relatives, Jesus showed that his mother was right in hoping that their efforts would fail; by indirectly rebuking them, he was secretly praising Mary for fulfilling the will of God. His words can be interpreted variously in accordance with the different attitudes of those for whom they were meant.

Happy are those who hear the word of God

The reply which he gave to the woman who declared that his mother was blessed can be interpreted in the same way, namely, as praise of Mary: "Shall we not say, Blessed are those who hear the word of God, and keep it?" [9] He emphasizes that the true greatness of Mary does not reside in the fact that she is a mother, but in that she is completely devoted to God. He protests against the false notion that Mary expected to derive any material advantage from her position as the mother of the Messias. A very human idea holds that a man who rises to a respectable and powerful position will naturally use his position to improve the lot of his family and of his friends. This idea was also applied by the Jews to the Messias, who would enjoy supreme power on earth; and this idea caused frequent disputes among the apostles as to who was destined to occupy the first place in his kingdom. The same idea was no doubt in the minds of his cousins when they urged him to show himself in public, so that they might benefit from his popularity.

[9] Luke 11:28.

51

But Christ consistently rejected all these attempts to derive advantage from the founding of the kingdom; he told his disciples that it belonged to the Father to assign each one his place, that no favoritism would be shown, and that nothing could be gained by scheming for first place. The only privilege he would grant to them was that of being more closely associated with his passion. When James and John were disputing about a place of honor, all he did was to indicate that they were destined to suffer with him. That was the only advantage he offered them.

He wished it to be clearly understood that there would be no concession to family interest in his kingdom, not even for the sake of his mother. Mary would enjoy no special right or favor with regard to anything which God condemned in others; she would not be permitted to enter the kingdom of heaven on easier terms than the others. The happiness which Christ had come into the world to offer mankind was subject to the same basic condition for all, including Mary: to hear the word of God and to keep it. The merit of the Blessed Virgin and the place she was destined to occupy in the kingdom were directly related to her faithfulness in following the word of God. Christ had no wish to spare his mother from any common obligation, for he allowed her to witness his terrible sufferings at the end. This unique privilege of taking an intimate and painful part in his passion was reserved for his mother, rather than for the apostles. This clearly shows that his love for her was not marred by any soft-heartedness. On the contrary, he wished all those who might be inclined to believe that he would be more indulgent to her than to others clearly to understand that his love was impartial and that he would not tolerate any exception to the divinely established rule, even for the sake of his beloved mother. By reminding them of this high requirement he paid a tribute to his mother, who had so admirably lived up to the condition. By placing her on a level with all other human beings he raised her above the level of them all.

His praise must be discovered

The words of Christ which have been preserved in the Gospels certainly do not give the impression that he was wont to display devotion to his mother; instead, his devotion has to be gathered from his various acts in the course of his life. Some of the things which he said seem to imply a rebuke, or a rebuff, or disregard for her; a closer examination of the context shows that these same words imply approval, praise, and the desire to associate her more closely with his work. The reader who contents himself with a first impression is easily put off the track; reflection enables him to realize that Mary is really being praised and that this praise is all the more effective because it is conveyed in such a subtle way. The relation between Mary and Jesus will only be comprehensible to the person who tries to understand the language of their hearts, a much more subtle means of communication than the language of the lips. Christ observes this discretion to the very end. There is no solemn pronouncement when from the cross he declares that Mary is to become the mother of all mankind. He simply says to those who are most immediately concerned, to Mary and to the well-beloved disciple: "Woman, this is thy son." [10] We are allowed to guess the full meaning of this phrase and interpret it as an expression of the universal motherhood of Mary. Jesus clearly and emphatically states that his Father is the Father of all Christians, but he only hints, as it were, at the fact that Mary is the mother of all his followers. The reason for this lies in the fact that the unique and transcendent nature of his relations with the Father requires that he be as explicit on this point as he possibly can, whereas his relations with his mother belong to the sphere of human relationships, which are easier to understand and can therefore be expressed more indirectly. The Father forms the center of his revelation and must therefore appear in broad daylight. So as not to interfere with the light which he is anxious to concentrate on the Father and on himself, he allows Mary to remain in the shadows. But Christ's words nevertheless betray his desire to exalt the splendor of his mother; and the filial instincts of men, inspired by the example of Christ himself and by the Holy Spirit, will lose no time in uncovering this hidden treasure and proclaiming the true greatness of Mary.

[10] John 19:26.

Intimacy

We are now able to get a better picture of the filial heart of Christ and of the development of his love for his mother. This development begins and is pursued in the quiet atmosphere of Nazareth. Nazareth is the scene of an intimate relationship between two human hearts, a relationship unique in the history of the world, one marked by few words and much silence and nourished by the ordinary acts of love. Rather than call it a relationship between two hearts, we should perhaps say that there was a gradual moulding of the heart of Jesus under the influence of his mother's love, for it was the tremendous task of Mary to mould the human heart of the Son of God. This heart was formed physically in the womb of Mary and began to beat there, but it was developed psychologically under the influence of her love. The function of Mary was somewhat analogous to that of the Father; it was from the Father that Jesus received his divine love and it was from Mary that he directly received his human heart. The tender affection with which the Word looks at the Father and never ceases contemplating him and being absorbed in him from all eternity was reproduced in Jesus as a child in the intimate and loving way in which his child's heart was turned towards its mother. The baby eyes of Jesus were fixed on Mary, gazed at her, and drank in her presence, in the same way that the attention of the Word is fixed on the countenance of the Father. The smile which appeared on his lips whenever he saw his mother was

55

a continuation of his eternal smile at the face of the
Father. We know that Jesus was fond of discovering
signs of the Father's loving care in nature and in men
in the course of his public life; he noticed this especially in the case of the birds and the flowers, but he
was above all fond of discovering faith in the souls of
men. Whose soul could have reminded him of the
love of the Father better than the soul of his mother?
Like the Father himself, she had brought him forth
into the world while preserving her virginity, and the
divine love which inspired her soul was reflected in her
demeanor and in everything she did. Whenever Jesus
looked at her with his innocent, childlike eyes, he must
have been amazed to find the Father there. Her different moods were an astonishing reminder of the
Father's moods; her words recalled the thoughts heard
before only in the intimacy of heaven; her silence revived the memory of the Father's silence. Everything
about the Blessed Virgin recalled the Father and reminded him of his love. If Jesus later rejoiced in the
Holy Spirit with admiration for the way in which the
Father directed certain souls towards him, it is logical
to suppose that he was overjoyed to discover in Mary's
every act evidence of this intimate and remarkable
presence of the Father. The constant rediscovery of
the Father transformed his everyday life with Mary
into a continual surprise. This continual development
of his mother's affection for him served to prolong the
embrace of the Father, so that his filial attitude towards the Father hardly had to be modified at all in
being directed towards his mother.

Yet there was a highly important difference between these two filial attitudes. In his relations with the Father the human heart of Jesus had only to follow the filial devotion of the Word in the course of his earthly existence, but in his relations with Mary the very opposite was true; her mother's heart had first to be moulded by the divine love of the Word before it could be assigned the task of forming the human heart of Jesus. Mary thus received everything from her Son, on condition that she give everything back to him. We can now see that their intimate relationship had an exceptionally profound meaning, in that it began before the conception of Jesus when the Blessed Virgin entrusted herself to the divine power for the purpose of being prepared for her rôle as his mother. There was thus established between future mother and Son a sort of pre-harmony. We can likewise understand how extremely humble Christ was in being willing to allow himself to be educated by her, after he had, as God, formed the heart of his mother. The Master indeed became the pupil. When the Gospel tells us that Jesus was subject as a child to his parents, it refers to this paradoxical situation of a divine person submitting himself to be schooled by human beings whom he had himself created and formed.

Maternal education and love of the Father

This submission was very profound and Mary was therefore in a position to exercise a more decisive influence on the heart of Jesus than any other mother in the case of her child. The education of Jesus is of course not exclusively the work of Mary; Christ possessed within himself an inner principle, his divine nature, which guided the development of all his faculties and various activities. The Word expressed itself in the human nature which it had assumed. We shall endeavor to explain later how the heart of Jesus reveals the Father himself and how the Word is the perfect image of the Father. The part played by divine causation in the development of the child of Nazareth is essential, but it does not exclude the contribution of Mary, which is also essential. The divine nature of the Word was pleased to assume a human nature with the help of a human mother. It is this function of the Blessed Virgin in connection with the education of the human heart of Jesus that we wish to examine now; it will help us to understand the mystery of his Incarnation.

It was the mother of Jesus who fostered in his human heart the development of his deepest affection: his love for the Father. This is uniquely paradoxical; he who loved the Father from all eternity learned to love him in a human way at the hands of his mother. We have pointed out how Jesus discovered the divine countenance of the Father in the features and gestures of Mary. It is a remarkable thing that the Blessed Virgin herself helped him to make this discovery. In common with all mothers, she assumed the responsibility of developing in her child a love for the heavenly Father and the growth of pious thoughts. She taught her Son the human way to honor the Father and human forms of worship. She taught him, who was the Master of prayer, how to pray. Jesus humbly went to school at her hands and learned how to pronounce the name of God. In future years, when the fervor of his prayer will so impress his disciples that they ask him to teach them how to pray, he will simply give a permanent form to the devotional thoughts he learned from his mother. The prayer he taught the apostles emphasized the things which were uppermost in the mind of Mary: the honoring of God and furtherance of his kingdom. Did she not say to the angel: "Behold the handmaid of the Lord; let it be unto me according to thy word"? [11] Her reply on this occasion foreshadowed the requests which were later incorporated in the first part of the Our Father. The second part of this prayer also reflected the thoughts of Mary. The Blessed Virgin had no more reason to ask divine forgiveness for her own sins than had her Son, since she was completely pure; but the granting of daily bread, the forgiveness of the sins of others, and freedom from the many afflictions which beset humanity were legitimate concerns of hers which she especially desired to recommend to God. Was she not anxious to promote good will by setting an example herself in forgiving the injuries which she received from others? Every request in the Our Father bore the mark of the Blessed Virgin; Jesus translated into words thoughts which she had already had and which she had communicated to him. His sublime prayer during his agony in the gar-

[11] Luke 1:38.

59

den: "Father . . . only as thy will is, not as mine is," [12] had no doubt been heard on the lips of his mother and he was induced to repeat it at this critical moment in his life, just as we are wont to repeat things which we have learned in our childhood at critical moments in our lives, things, very often, which have been taught us by our mothers.

Did not Mary fill Jesus with a preference for prayer which springs from the heart rather than from the lips? Unlike the Pharisees who were given to repeating long prayers in public, Mary was discreet in her devotions and was used to praying with her whole soul. When Jesus advised his disciples not to use too many words and to withdraw when they prayed, may he not have been suggesting that they follow the example of his mother? She was the one who instilled in him his love for silent prayer; whenever he withdrew during the course of his public life to pray in silence, he probably had a feeling that he was recapturing the atmosphere of Nazareth.

The Blessed Virgin also gave to her child a sense of moderation in religious matters; the religious sentiments of Jesus were very strong, but he maintained a sense of balance and moderation in expressing them. Just as Mary was sometimes inspired with great joy to sing the praises of God, as she did in the *Magnificat*, so Jesus sometimes trembled in the Holy Spirit when he was carried away by love for the Father. But these outbursts of joy were always simple and dignified; in

[12] Luke 22:42.

general it can be said that Christ was restrained in expressing his feelings of devotion.

Jesus must also have received from his mother his unshakable confidence in prayer. Mary taught Jesus what she herself believed so fervently, that one must have complete confidence in the goodness of God and never grow weary of asking him for a favor. The heavenly Father is unable to resist those who persist in asking him for anything. That is why she will never lose hope and will continue to pray even after the shameful death of her Son on the cross. The resurrection was in effect his marvelous way of answering her prayers. Jesus continually tells his disciples that those who persevere in prayer will eventually be rewarded, and illustrates his teaching by the example of the poor, weak widow who finally obtains satisfaction from a judge whom she had long entreated. It is possible that Jesus had in mind in the case of this widow the example of his mother, who was weak and defenseless from the human point of view, but mighty with God because of her perseverance in prayer.

The occasions on which he was moved to give thanks to the Father and refer all glory to him for his work as the Messias also were inspired by the example of his mother. Could Mary, who was inspired with the beautiful sentiments of the *Magnificat* when she heard the news of the Incarnation, have failed to instill in her Son the belief that all things can be accomplished by the power of God and that he should be praised for his benefits and blessings? Mary's inclination to consider the events of her life as a kind of hymn of praise was imparted to her Son. It is an amazing thought, but the human love of Christ for the Father, which was partly the inspiration for everything he did, was developed in him by his mother. The Blessed Virgin had the extremely delicate task of intervening in the intimate relationship between Father and Son, so that a human heart could be formed in Jesus in perfect accord with the divine love. All the intimate thoughts of Christ, his complete devotion to the Father, his praise and admiration for the Father, his desire to serve him and his feeling of gratitude towards him, his confidence in the Father's goodness, the sincerity of his prayers to the Father, his continual communion with the Father, all these developed in Jesus as a result of the instruction which he received at the hands of his mother. Christ was indebted to Mary for that which he prized above all else, for she was the one who taught him to love the Father.

Maternal education and love of mankind

Jesus is indebted to his mother not only for the development of his human love for the Father; the vast treasury of his love for men, which will be expended so generously in the course of his public life, was also stored up in him under his mother's inspiration, and her hand can be seen in the many different ways in which this love will be expressed.

Mary was the one who inspired Christ with the general principle which governed his whole public life:

to conquer through love. This is the way she behaved, if we may judge from the scant information furnished by the Gospels. Her love was humble, patient, and absolutely unshakable on all occasions. Her regard for the guests at Cana was what caused her to intervene in a matter of secondary importance and produced the miracle. The steadfastness of her love no doubt gradually had an effect on the cousins of Jesus who had originally refused to believe in his Messianic rôle, for we find that they had apparently changed their minds when they gathered with her and the others in the cenacle before Pentecost. She could have refused to have anything to do with them in view of their unbelief, which was no doubt a source of anxiety to her; but instead she clung to them with greater devotion than ever, for we find her in their company when they come to see Jesus. This persistent good will on her part must have overcome their resistance and caused them to share her belief in her Son. Mary clearly showed that her faith was unshakable when she took her position at the foot of his cross, after he had been abandoned by the others. She is the one who inspired Jesus with his persistence in love which enabled him to struggle to the very end. His policy will be to attract men to himself by persisting in loving them. When he invited the rich young man to sell all his goods and to follow him, he looked into his eyes with an expression of love which those who witnessed the scene were never to forget. He looked at the young man in the same way Mary had frequently looked at him, with a heart full of a mother's love. Jesus would, like his mother, be careful not to break off relations with his enemies and would strive to keep alive the spark that might still be burning there. Why did he not banish Judas from his presence? Because Mary had taught him never to despair of love and to cling to souls more obstinately the more hard-hearted they seemed to be. That is why he did not refuse to engage in discussion with the Pharisees and consented to answer their insidious questions. By asking for their forgiveness at Calvary he would show that he had not ceased to love them even then.

Although Jesus was prepared to go to all lengths in his effort to win men's souls, he was never willing to exercise any kind of pressure in this regard, even that kind of pressure which is sometimes felt to be necessary for the good of those concerned. The rich young man was allowed to do as he pleased and no force was used to save Judas in spite of himself. This reserve in love and respect for individual liberty were traits which Jesus derived from his mother in the human order of causation. There were certain indications which seemed to show that she had been careful not to stunt her child's growth by a too imperious or too monopolizing mother's love. Her Son was perfectly submissive to her, but she never abused this submission. She resisted the temptation to which so many mothers succumb of watching over their children so jealously and guarding them so closely that they interfere with the child's normal development.

She took care to promote the spontaneous development of Jesus. When he was found in the temple, she refrained from judging his conduct on the spot and simply asked him: "My Son, why hast thou treated us so?" She was not rebuking him for disobedience, but simply expressing the anguish which she and Joseph felt: "Think, what anguish of mind thy father and I have endured, searching for thee." [13] It should be noted that she did not attempt to discipline him in any way, but allowed him to explain his action in any way he chose; she reminded him of the fact that he had never desired to cause his parents any trouble in the past and thereby suggested the nature of his reply. Mary likewise refrained from asking her Son openly to perform the miracle at Cana. She was content to bring the awkward situation to his attention: "They have no more wine." Her desire was certainly apparent and Jesus immediately grasped this, but she refrained from putting her thoughts into words in order to avoid the impression of bringing any pressure to bear on him. It was for Jesus himself to consider the matter and decide what should be done. His reply was apparently discouraging, so she preserved her Son's freedom of action by simply saying to the servants: "Do whatever he tells you." [14] Her love for Jesus was too great to allow her to impose upon him. She was not one of those mothers who treat their grown sons as if they were completely at their service. Her intervention was very discreet; she was careful not

[13] Luke 2:48.   [14] John 2:5.

to say anything which might hamper his freedom and allowed him to reject her suggestion, if he had so desired. This attitude of discretion and respect for others was characteristic of the way in which she had brought Jesus up; it was modified in accordance with the various stages of his development and more strongly emphasized the older he grew. She succeeded in convincing him that love cannot be forced on the person who is loved. Christ would win the love of men because they would be attracted to his person and his teaching of their own free will; he would appeal to the spontaneous expression of their love.

Other remarkable traits of his heart are apparently also due to Mary. Jesus shows that he is fond of the poor and of sinners. He is moved by the sight of bodily suffering and eagerly cures these ills by miracles. He is even more moved by spiritual suffering and looks for those who are sinners in order to bring them back into the fold. It is from his mother that a child ordinarily learns to show sympathy for the misfortunes of others. In the case of Mary we have only one example of this sort of sympathy, when she saved the bride and groom at the wedding feast from the embarrassment occasioned by their poverty; but we may readily assume that she had a sympathetic heart and passed this trait on to her Son.

Christ's simplicity also seems to have been inherited from his mother. Jesus presented the Jews and mankind with a complete paradox in the simplicity of his behavior as the Messias, who was supposed to be a great revolutionary and liberator. Contrary to their expectations, he never stood on dignity as a barrier between himself and others, and it was always so easy to approach him that people were simply unaware of the great distance between man and God. He avoided anything which might serve to arouse a feeling of fear in his followers and showed that he was completely devoted to his friends. The mode of his life was simple and there was never any attempt to impress people by appearing to be what he was not. He conducted himself in the course of his public life as he had learned to do in his humble existence at Nazareth. The simplicity of Mary continued to inspire him on the cross, as we can see from the very human way in which he suffered and died. He showed his simplicity in a fondness for the things of nature. It is rather significant that he loved the lilies of the field, those ordinary flowers to be found everywhere in the countryside, and that he preferred them to the luxurious garments of Solomon. We can perhaps see in this preference a humble reminder of the days of his childhood, when he gathered such flowers to offer to his loving mother. These flowers perhaps represented the very image of his mother, who was an ordinary woman from all indications, but extraordinarily full of grace. Such simplicity of taste would be consistent with an outlook that was basically religious.

Connected with this attitude was the remarkable humility which the Blessed Virgin imparted to her Son. Nothing seems to have been more characteristic of her nature, as it is represented to us in the Gospels, than her gentle and humble heart. The authority of his mother, to which Jesus is obliged to submit as a child and as a young man, is a sweet yoke and an easy burden. He wishes to impose the same kind of yoke on his disciples. His mother set an example of service in the household; he places himself at the service of all men. His statement: "The Son of Man did not come to have service done him; he came to serve others," [15] no doubt reflects the thought which inspired his mother throughout her life of retirement. When she became the mother of the Messias through the agency of the Most High, her first impulse was to pay a visit to Elizabeth, to place herself at the service of her cousin. She who had been honored above all others with the privilege of divine motherhood was pleased to become the least of all by taking the humble rôle of a servant. Her gesture of humility will be repeated thirty years later when Jesus encounters the Baptist; her Visitation foreshadows the scene by the Jordan thirty years later, when Christ, fully aware of his greatness as the Messias, humbles himself before John and allows his precursor to baptize him. When Christ finds that his disciples are far too preoccupied with the question of who is to occupy the first place in the kingdom, he desires to teach them a lesson in humility and simply repeats the gesture he must have often seen his mother perform in their household. He girds himself with a towel, puts water into a basin, and

[15] Mark 10:45.

proceeds to wash the feet of his disciples. This simple act, which the rich normally leave to servants, was performed by Mary herself in her own home when she received guests. She was at once mistress and servant of her household. Though his disciples called him "Master" and "Lord," Jesus acted as servant to them, washing their feet and setting them an example of humility; he "knew well that the Father had left everything in his hands." [16] During his youth, Jesus must have been impressed when he saw his beloved mother bend down over her guests to wash their feet, for her example inspired him to do the same thing when he wished to set an example of humility.

Mary also passed on to Jesus his concern for the welfare of others, a welfare which was not confined to generalities, but extended to details and the humblest needs of the individual. A touching example of this is his attitude towards the disciples, who have just returned from their missionary work and are eager to give him a glowing account of all that they have accomplished. Jesus invites them to rest a while before listening to their account, just as a mother who is anxious to hear all about the trip which her son has taken advises him to rest before telling her the story. When Jairus and his wife look with amazement at their daughter who has just been raised from the dead, Jesus advises them to give her something to eat. On the shores of the sea of Tiberias after his resurrection Jesus himself prepares a meal for his disciples.

[16] John 13:3.

These acts of Christ reveal the influence of his mother's heart.

Finally, we may say that Jesus owes his emotional stability to his mother. On the one hand we find that he is quite strongly moved by some emotions; for example, he permits himself to weep on a number of occasions. He is also moved by pity, anger, disgust, fear, joy, sorrow, and amazement. He possesses the whole range of human emotions. On the other hand he maintains perfect control over all his emotions, never ceases to be governed by the will of the Father, and never permits his heart to lead him where he does not wish to go. In expressing his emotions he shows a remarkable sense of balance, which prevents him from allowing too much importance to be attached to them or making a display of them. He maintains an essential strength of character. It is largely through proper training at his mother's hands that a man successfully attains such a harmonious development of his emotional life. Mary showed both the great depth of her emotions and her control over them at the foot of his cross, and it was no doubt from her that Jesus derived the same characteristics.

Mary formed the heart of Christ more by what she was than by what she said; the love of Jesus developed quite naturally in accordance with the pattern of her love. He acquired from her his tireless energy, his profound respect for human liberty, the depth of his emotions, his control over them, his boundless solicitude for others, his accessibility, and his essential simplicity. He could lay claim to all his mother's characteristics without having to make any choice, for she constantly conformed herself to the will of the Father and the inspiration of the Holy Spirit to such an extent that there could not possibly be any divergence between her conduct and what Jesus expected from her. As a child at Nazareth he had only to open his soul to that of his mother and receive all that she could give him. He entrusted himself to Mary with complete confidence and allowed his character to be moulded by the gentle inspiration of her love.

Naturally, he already possessed the fulness of divine love. In emphasizing the human qualities of the education he received at his mother's hands we have no intention to deny or to disregard the part played by his divine nature; Christ formed himself at the same time that he permitted himself to be formed. But it was through the agency of Mary, a person eminently pleasing to God, that the Word chose to give himself his human heart.

The drama

Behind this perfect harmony between mother and Son which was never troubled by any sign of discord, a drama was gradually unfolding. It would be incomplete to speak of the idyllic atmosphere of Nazareth without mentioning a wound which existed in the midst of this peace and calm and was destined to develop along with it. The words of Simeon could not easily be forgotten. Mary had immediately recognized in the prophecy of this inspired old man the divine voice, the familiar voice of the Holy Spirit. The echo of these words lingered in her soul and stirred the innermost depths of her being. She kept the prophecy in her heart, tried to penetrate its mystery, tried to assume the proper attitude towards the great sorrow which was foreshadowed. Gradually the sword began to make the wound deeper. When she looked at her child with all the affection so natural to mothers, she could not help feeling that a threat hung over him. The more she delighted in looking at him, the more she was afraid of losing him. Her suffering, so to speak, increased with her happiness. Her apprehensions were suddenly intensified, when incidents like the loss of Jesus in Jerusalem or the threats of the Pharisees made her feel that the moment of trial might be at hand. "Will it be now?" she kept asking herself in anguish. All her happiness as a mother served only to keep alive this secret sorrow.

For his part Jesus felt the same kind of suffering in his filial love for his mother. He had come into this world for the moment of his passion and he knew perfectly well that his public ministry was destined to end in a catastrophe; but that was where the Father was leading him and that was the goal on which his heart was set. When he observed the care which his mother lavished on him, he could not keep from thinking that all this was destined to end in his condemnation and crucifixion; and in the face which leaned over him so affectionately he must have discerned the tears of Calvary. He would be the cause of weeping to those eyes which looked at him so ten-

derly. The peacefulness of Nazareth foreboded the
coming of a storm. Jesus not only foresaw all this, he
regarded it as his mission to prepare his mother for
her part in it. He was destined to enlarge the wound
which had been inflicted on the heart of Mary by the
words of Simeon.

He probably never told his mother clearly and
explicitly what would happen. Both were content to
suffer side by side in the secret of their hearts without
sharing the disappointments or thoughts which
troubled them. But Jesus occasionally referred by gesture or word to the trials which were to come, explained their general meaning, and prepared Mary for
the road which would lead to his sacrifice. His stay in
the temple at the age of twelve was designed to help
his mother appreciate beforehand the cruel separation
she would have to experience. We can readily imagine
what torture it must have been for the loving heart of
Jesus to have to make his mother suffer deliberately,
so that the divine plan for the redemption of mankind
could be carried out. He derived comfort from the
courageous way in which Mary bore all these trials
and entrusted herself to God.

She had another premonition of the anguish she
would feel at Calvary, when Jesus left Nazareth to
take up the work of his ministry. During the thirty
years in which he had remained in the village the lives
of Mary and Jesus had been so closely connected that
it would have been hard to separate them. When the
time for parting arrived, they must have felt that they
were being torn from each other and losing a vital part

73

of themselves. This leave-taking, of course, did not exclude the possibility of a happier future, but this did not prevent the sorrow from being felt. As so often happens when a son departs to take up his sacred calling, the parents are the ones who make the heavier sacrifice; the son is usually so thrilled by what he is about to do that he is hardly aware of any sacrifice at all, even at the moment of parting. But the devotion of Jesus to Mary was so deep-rooted and his capacity for understanding the least movements of her heart was so marked, that he deeply felt the sadness this parting must have caused her and was moved by her suffering. He was less sorry for himself than he was for her. He no doubt concealed his sadness under a show of courage and joy. While he secretly admired his mother's strength of character, he openly expressed his gratitude for all that he had received from her. How could one who was later to show how much he was touched by all expressions of gratitude, who would mildly begrudge the fact that he had been thanked by only one of the ten lepers whom he had healed, fail to thank his mother on such an occasion as this? He realized that all the traits of character which would help him in the work of his ministry were the result of training at her hands. He was now about to impart to mankind what his mother had already implanted in his soul and in his heart. The one who was always so eager to render thanks to the heavenly Father for all his gifts could not have failed to convey his gratitude to Mary. We have used the word "convey" advisedly, for it is difficult to express this kind of gratitude in words and usually not a good idea to be too explicit in these matters. Jesus simply showed his mother by suitable word and gesture that he was profoundly grateful for all the love and affection she had lavished on him in preparing him for his rôle as a man and as the Messias, and also for the final sacrifice which was destined to crown the work of her education.

This feeling of sorrow in her heart was revived again at Cana. While he generously granted her request on this occasion and approved her intervention by performing the miracle, he recalled their separation by the words: "Woman, why dost thou trouble me with that?" [17] These words inaugurated the rôle of Mary as the Mediatrix of all graces, but at the same time served to remind her of the sacrifice she must be prepared to face in assuming this rôle. When he later told the crowd that he belonged to them rather than to his mother, he again re-opened the wound in her heart. Although we realize that the Blessed Virgin on this occasion was in full agreement with the sentiments of her Son and wished him to be firm in his reply as a warning to the other members of her family, these words of his tended to accentuate her sacrifice. Christ was well aware of his mother's anguish at the time, but was forced to trample on his filial regard for her because of the important issue involved.

Finally, the hour arrived for which Jesus had so

[17] John 2:4.

75

carefully prepared his mother. As a matter of fact she had been fearing the worst for some time, ever since the Pharisees began threatening his life. Hence, when she walked beside her Son on the road to Calvary, her anguish was not something which suddenly developed, but burst forth like an overripe fruit. We have already pointed out that the most intense sorrow felt by Christ on the cross was his feeling of abandonment by the Father. Next to this, he was most distressed by the sight of his mother standing beside him and experiencing all the anguish which filled her heart. If Christ could only have spared her that, if he could only have calmed the throbbing of her heart and dried those tears! But what could he do, nailed to the cross by the will of the Father? He could do nothing to relieve the anguish of her heart. He whose heart was so full of tenderness and gratitude was obliged to punish the being who was dearest to him in the whole world. The sight of his mother's inflamed eyes must have pierced him more terribly than his consuming thirst or the mockery of his enemies.

Just as he was more closely united with the Father during this hour of abandonment, the suffering of his mother served to bind him more closely to her. Jesus felt that he was Mary's son more deeply on the cross than he ever had before; this was the supreme test of their love for each other. This terrible experience, by uniting them in the hour of trial, bound them together more intimately than all the peaceful and quiet years in Nazareth ever could have done.

This final act of the drama gives meaning to the

whole development of his filial regard for his mother. Christ was obliged to separate himself from her more and more because of the work of redemption, but this very fact caused him to draw still closer to her. The anguish which he caused her heart united him with her more completely and intimately than ever before. Mother and Son were destined to be brought together in the suffering of love.

Christ consecrated this separation from a mother whom he dearly loved when he designated Mary as the mother of mankind. He wished all men to benefit from the tender care of a mother who had lovingly watched over him while he was growing up and now had taken her stand at the foot of his cross. He claimed from her as an ultimate sacrifice her acceptance of the apostle John in place of the Son whom she dearly loved and required that she devote herself henceforth to sons who were not her own and could never take the place in her heart of the one she was now losing. Jesus wished to suffer the emptiness of death in the affection of his mother before suffering it on the cross. Yet, by causing Mary to be thus united and associated with his final sacrifice, and by tearing her from himself in order to give her to us, he succeeded in binding her more closely to himself by the rôle she was destined to play in the work of redemption and by the assistance which she would provide in helping him realize the thought dearest to his heart: the salvation of all men. Mary would henceforth have the extremely important task of being the mother of men in applying the gifts of redemption to them; mother and Son would be intimate collaborators in the work of salvation. Jesus would be drawn to his mother even more by her part in contributing to the sanctification of men; all the love which he felt for men would thus serve to strengthen his love for his mother.

At the same time he also began the glorification of his mother. After saying to her: "Woman, this is thy son," he said to the well-beloved apostle: "This is thy mother." [18] He wished the apostle to feel the love and respect for Mary which is reserved for a mother and thus laid the foundations for Christian devotion to the Blessed Virgin, a devotion destined to assume tremendous proportions in later generations. When he gave his mother to men, he charged them with the responsibility of honoring and venerating her and of proclaiming her beauty and greatness. His followers need not be restrained, as he was, in giving expression to their admiration and love for his mother.

Christ was able to compensate himself for this restraint and give free expression to his desire to honor his mother only after her death. He permitted his mother to remain on earth for a while to establish her function as the mother of mankind and to allow her to preside over the foundation and first progress of his Church. Then he gathered her to himself again in the assumption of her body and soul, and, by putting an end to their painful separation, was free at last, for all eternity, to speak of the joy and wonder felt by his filial heart.

[18] John 19:26, 27.

78

3. HEART DEVOTED TO MEN

When one of the scribes or Pharisees asked Jesus what commandment of the Law was most important, our Master was not content to reply that we should love God with our whole heart. He added that there was, in addition to the first commandment, a second one like unto the first: we should also love our neighbor. He thus made it clear that love of God and neighbor are mutually inclusive and presuppose each other; this is what makes them equally important and "like" each other. There is no way to love God without loving neighbor, and no way to love neighbor without loving God.

Jesus' statement regarding the commandments reveals the true purpose of his life; he embodied those commandments himself before giving them to men. There is a love for men in the heart of Jesus "like" his love for the Father. Both these loves are, in him, identical, because he expresses his love for the Father by means of his loving devotion to men. It was for the sake of men and their salvation that the Son accepted the mission assigned him by his Father; it was on their behalf that he left the Father and came into the world, because he himself informed us that he was leaving the world to return to the Father. If men had not needed someone to save them, the Incarnation would have been robbed of all meaning; the Word need not have appeared on earth in order to love the Father and to love him fully. He could have remained in the intimacy of heaven and continued to carry on his eternal conversation of love with the Father without any disturbance. But men existed, men whom he had himself created; and they could not be an object of indifference in his sight. They caused him to appear on earth; for their sake the Word became Christ. His love for men was what caused him to assume a human heart; before being a source of love, this heart was a result of love.

The human heart of Christ was created by God to be at the service of mankind; it must therefore undergo training in all the ways of human love in the calm atmosphere of Nazareth. We know nothing about the details of this training except the results: Christ showed an affection for men which he had learned in the seclusion of Nazareth. It is difficult for us to appreciate from the little information provided by the Gospels the true scope of this love, because love depends upon personal contact for expression and no book can hope to recreate all the variable factors which are apt to play an important part in such contacts. We may try to recapture some of them, however, and examine the way in which Christ applies this principle, which governs his whole life. All his actions, from his baptism and withdrawal into the desert to his death and final resurrection, are inspired by his love for mankind. If it is true that none of his acts, attitudes, thoughts or emotions has any source other than his love of the Father, it is no less true that these can only be explained by his love for men. Even those acts wherein this love is not immediately apparent are inspired by it. When Christ allows himself to be baptized by John, he does not do so for his own benefit, for he is absolutely pure and has no need of conversion or penance; it is motivated by his love for men. For men does he permit the devil to approach him and tempt him in the desert, because the stake involved is the salvation of mankind. By letting Peter, James, and John behold his glory in the Transfiguration, he wishes to stimulate their courage in view of his coming passion. His carefully planned appearances after the resurrection show that he triumphed over death not for the sake of impressing men, but in order to share with them his new joy and new life. Even his ascension, his final return to the Father, is motivated by his love for men; he makes it clear to his disciples that he is ascending into heaven in order to prepare a place for them.

By discovering this inspiration of love in the events of Jesus' life and by appreciating the way in which every act and word of his is influenced by it we are able to get at the true meaning of his Gospel and revelation. Christ came to earth for the express purpose of showing us his love. As in the case of every true manifestation of love, his love must be discovered by those for whom it is meant. His love is enveloped in a kind of veil; if it were too obvious, it would seem more like pride and would prevent the free expression of men's love instead of promoting it; it would repel souls instead of winning them. His love must therefore be discovered. Those who prefer to ignore it and avoid all recognition of it are of course free to do so; those who endeavor to pierce this veil and find out what is underneath discover that his love assumes the tremendous proportions that it actually has, and that under a surface which often seems ordinary and uninteresting there are bewildering depths.

THE GOOD SHEPHERD

In order to help us understand this love for men which possessed the heart of Christ, St. John has preserved the allegory of the good shepherd among the teachings of the Master. Jesus begins one of his sermons by proposing that his disciples consider the example of the good shepherd.[1] With the simple and direct manner of one who derived his knowledge of men from first-hand impressions, he describes the behavior of the shepherd with his sheep, tells of the familiar way in which he calls each one by name, leads them out of the fold, and walks before them on the road. To stress the superiority of the shepherd's behavior, he contrasts his attitude with that of the thief,

[1] John 10:11–18.

82

brigand or hireling. Thieves and brigands do not enter the sheepfold by the gate, but endeavor to steal and slaughter the sheep. They wish to kill the sheep, whereas the shepherd would have them live, would fatten them, and would make them prosper in the hope that they may have life and have it more abundantly. The sheep refuse to follow the brigands whose voices are unfamiliar to them, but they confidently obey the voice of the shepherd who leads them to green pastures. As for the hirelings, the flock does not belong to them and they show no concern for it; they act out of pure self-interest. When the hour of danger arrives, the contrast between the hireling and shepherd is striking; the hireling flees before the wolf, but the shepherd lays down his life, if need be, for the sake of the sheep. The disciples were probably charmed by the freshness of the picture their Master drew for them, but could not understand what he was driving at. They presumably asked Jesus to explain the meaning of the allegory to them; the Gospel does not mention their question, but we may assume that they asked it, because this is their usual reaction whenever he delivers a sermon of such nature. Christ ordinarily begins by telling a story, then he waits for his hearers to ask questions about the lesson he has been trying to convey. On this occasion he answers their question by giving them a splendid definition of himself: "I am the good shepherd." [2] He passes from allegory to mystery.

[2] John 10:11.

We have briefly noticed the context of this important statement, because it reveals the wholly simple and natural way in which Jesus communicates the most sublime and essential truths. He explains truths very dear to his own heart without giving his hearers the impression that he is saying anything of great importance at all. He has a faculty for making the sublime seem so humble! There is nothing new in his description of the shepherd; it is borrowed from everyday life. The shepherd's rôle was certainly not one of the most honored professions; shepherds were rather crude people who were obliged to live somewhat apart from the rest of humanity, and the inhabitants of the towns and villages of Palestine no doubt looked down upon them. By comparing himself with a shepherd Jesus is certainly not attempting to exalt himself in the eyes of his disciples, and yet in this humble comparison he does manage to reveal to them the essence of his heart.

The One who calls the sheep by name

Above all the good shepherd knows his sheep. He calls them by name. This may seem to be an insignificant detail, but it reveals the whole climate of his thought. A flock is a flock, as far as the casual passer-by is concerned; all the sheep look alike and seem to have the same importance. For the shepherd, however, each sheep has its own distinguishing characteristics and name. The shepherd knows his sheep perfectly, because he loves them and is personally interested in

84

each one. How lovingly he pronounces the names by which he chooses to call them! The first time he meets Peter, Jesus tells him: "Thou art Simon the son of Jona." [3] The name "Simon" will recur on the lips of the Lord with varying accents as he expresses the different moods of his love for the apostle: when he asks for friendly advice: "Simon . . . tell us what thou thinkest; on whom do earthly kings impose customs and taxes?" [4]; when he congratulates him: "Blessed art thou, Simon son of Jona; it is not flesh and blood, it is my Father in heaven that has revealed this to thee" [5]; when he promises to be at his side: "Simon, Simon, behold, Satan has claimed power over you all, so that he can sift you like wheat: but I have prayed for thee, that thy faith may not fail . . ." [6] Jesus pronounces the name of the chief of his disciples twice on this occasion in order to attach him more closely to himself and prevent him from being discouraged by his coming denial. Again we find Jesus sadly reproaching Peter: "Simon, art thou sleeping?" [7] Yet again we see Christ three times asking Peter for his love: "Simon, son of John, dost thou care for me?" [8] Not by chance alone is the name of the greatest of his disciples found so often on his lips in connection with expressions of love. He also delights in calling the others by name. Shortly before his death he endeavors to make Philip realize the importance of the intimacy he has

---

[5] Matt. 16:17.
[3] John 1:42.
[4] Matt. 17:24–25.

[6] Luke 22:31–32.
[7] Mark 14:37.
[8] John 21:15, 16, 17.

85

granted his apostles, the significance of which has largely escaped them: "What, Philip, . . . here am I, who have been all this while in your company; hast thou not learned to recognize me yet?" [9] In pronouncing that name for the last time, Jesus wishes to let Philip know how dearly he loves him. The last words he addresses to his betrayer include the mention of his name: "Judas, wouldst thou betray the Son of Man with a kiss?" [10] At Bethany the distraught Martha hears him say: "Martha, Martha, how many cares and troubles thou hast!" [11] The repetition of her name serves to make her think. Even the dead are called by name: "Lazarus, come out here." [12] Jesus speaks to his old friend in the same familiar tone he used when he was being entertained in his house; on this occasion his words summon his friend back to life; the voice of the good shepherd carries beyond the grave. Christ first addresses Mary Magdalen in an impersonal tone when he speaks to her after his resurrection: "Woman . . . why art thou weeping?" Then he calls her by name: "Mary." [13] The mention of her name, as if by magic, affects her immediately and suffices to renew all the close ties of love which had been so tragically interrupted by his death. Mary Magdalen was never to forget how Christ pronounced her name on this occasion; his voice was not only familiar but brought back to mind all the kindnesses he had shown her. The same voice will later be heard on the road to

[9] John 14:9.
[10] Luke 22:48.
[11] Luke 10:41.

[12] John 11:43.
[13] John 20:15, 16.

Damascus: "Saul, Saul, why dost thou persecute me?" [14] His persecutor is also called by name. After blinding him by his light and casting him to the ground, Jesus succeeds in winning over his former enemy by speaking to him in a familiar and friendly way. The apostle is destined never to forget the repetition of his name on this occasion; it symbolizes the love Christ has willed to extend to him.

These examples show how deeply the good shepherd was moved by love when he called his sheep by name. It shows what effect this had on them: Lazarus was recalled to life; Mary Magdalen ceased to be sad and was filled with joy and gladness; and Saul was transformed from a persecutor into a great apostle with a new name, Paul. Jesus sometimes marked the solemnity of the occasion by assigning a new name, as he did in the case of his favorite disciples Peter, James, and John; he gave them names which were related to their future rôles: "Peter" and "Sons of thunder."

The one who knows their hearts

Knowing a name is knowing a mere symbol. What Jesus knows in men is the entire personality with all its secret thoughts. While others see only the external appearance of those whom they chance to meet, the Lord is at once aware of the entire personality and life-story of those whom he happens to encounter. The eyes of men can conceal no thoughts from him, and he is able at once to recognize from

[14] Acts 9:4.

physical appearances the most profound tendencies and aspirations of a person. His look pierces the mystery of hearts.

Jesus knows his disciples from the first moment he calls them. He sees Nathanael coming towards him and says: "Here comes one who belongs to the true Israel; there is no falsehood in him." "How dost thou know me?" the latter asks him in surprise. "I saw thee when thou wast under the fig-tree, before Philip called thee." [15] He has always known those whom he chooses; he knows their character as well as the most insignificant facts about their lives, such as the fact that they were under a fig-tree. He knows them, because he sees them. The Samaritan woman experienced this knowledge. She thought that she could take refuge in her self-respect and maintain a barrier between herself and this Jew. But Christ pursues her as she endeavors to retreat and in one word reveals the true status of her moral life. "Sir, I perceive that thou art a prophet," [16] the woman replies as she feels completely found out. How often Jesus shows that he is capable of seeing through the hidden motives of his hearers, whether it be his disciples or the Pharisees. It is not necessary for his adversaries to give overt expression to their thoughts; according to the Gospel Jesus "answers" them, that is to say, he replies not to any words which they have expressed but to the thoughts in their hearts. For example, when the Pharisees fall to reasoning among themselves after he forgives the sins of the

[15] John 1:47–48. [16] John 4:19.

lame man, he answers: "Why do you reason thus in
your hearts?" [17] When Simon the Pharisee, in whose
house Jesus is dining, reflects that a prophet should
know that the woman who has thrown herself at his
feet is a sinner, Jesus tells him: "Simon, I have a word
for thy hearing." [18] Of his disciples, who had been disputing among themselves along the way as to who
should be the greatest, Jesus asks, upon their arrival at
Capharnaum: "What was the dispute you were holding on the way?" [19] His disciples are silent, but he
points to the example of a small child in order to solve
the question they have raised. Nothing escapes his sensitive, keen perception. He is aware that a woman has
touched him, a woman lost in the crowd pressing him
in on all sides, and he realizes that she has done so
under the inspiration of faith. Judas strives in vain to
keep his intentions secret; Jesus, knowing the gradual
development of that treachery in the heart of Judas,
repeatedly warns of what is about to occur: "And one
of you is a devil." [20] "Believe me, one of you is to betray me." [21] Hyprocrisy is helplessly unable to keep
the darkness of treachery from the light of his mind.

This penetrating knowledge enables Jesus to give
personal, intimate, and appropriate attention to each
person he meets. The first two disciples, who are unwilling to follow him immediately, seek further information by asking him where he lives. To them he

[17] Luke 5:22.
[18] Luke 7:40.
[19] Mark 9:33.

[20] John 6:71.
[21] John 13:21.

says: "Come and see." [22] By such an answer he allows
them to see for themselves and make up their own
minds before deciding to become his followers. The
publican Levi, on the other hand, receives an immediate summons: "Follow me." [23] Jesus requires from
some an immediate and definite abandonment of possessions, livelihood and parents; they are asked to sell
their goods, forbidden to return to the plough or to
their houses or to bury the dead. But we note that
Peter returned to his parents several times, and even
resumed his occupation of fishing on several occasions.
Nathanael, naturally frank, is attached to Christ from
the very moment when he hears what Jesus has to say
to him. The Samaritan woman, on the other hand, a
bit wary and inclined to dissimulation, must be
handled more carefully; he can only reveal himself to
her gradually. Before raising Lazarus, he demands an
act of faith from Martha and Mary, which he did not
demand from the widow of Naim. Though he tests
the faith of the Chanaanite woman, he encourages
and supports the faith of the wife of Jairus. In other
words, he knows how to deal with each soul in the
most suitable way.

Knowledge and sympathy

Penetrating as is Christ's knowledge, it is still the
knowledge a shepherd has of his sheep. The way in
which Jesus penetrates the innermost secrets of a person is the same as the cold, inquisitive way in which

22 John 1:39.   23 Mark 2:14.

90

a psychologist analyzes the state of a patient's mind and tries to discover the hidden motives of human conduct. The psychologist tries to be dispassionate and objective in his inquiry; he endeavors to analyze the patient's mind, judge it with reference to certain norms, and control it in accordance with the methods of his science. He tends to limit reactions to certain well-defined patterns, label various dispositions or individual characteristics, and finally deprive the personality of everything that is most unique or original about it, its mystery. In reality he does not succeed in probing into the real depths of the personality and reaching that spontaneous principle which is hidden from the eyes of all but God. This ultimate principle is apparent to Christ, but he does not attempt to look at one's personality coldly and objectively in order to control it for purposes of analysis or evaluation. He is moved to examine it through sympathy, and he will only penetrate a heart when he has been invited to do so through love; when he does enter the depths of a soul, he is extremely careful not to disturb or to violate its mystery. He never attempts to force his way in, he never injures anyone by his power of insight, he never employs his knowledge as a means of dominating souls in a tyrannical fashion. All souls, so intimately known by Christ, receive from him infinite respect, even those who resist him and are obstinate in their resistance. We find no evidence that he ever gazed upon his enemies in an attempt to overwhelm them by the might of his countenance, or stripped them of their thoughts by his omniscient powers, or rid himself of them by sudden and curt remarks. He could have used the knowledge he had of his opponents in his disputes with them; he could have brutally unmasked the thoughts they entertained in their hearts, humiliated them and overwhelmed them in shame. He rebuked them collectively, but only for attitudes which could by judged on their merits by anyone. He never cast a Pharisee's past sins in his face. In answering the malicious questions of these quibblers he could easily have had the better of them by alluding to certain failings on their part, failings that would have made them blush and hide themselves in shame. In the course of his trial he could have won an easy victory over Annas and Caiphas by giving the court an account of their lives. When he was brought before these persons, both of whom had been involved in dubious affairs and continued to derive illegal profits from their position, Christ could have accused them of their wrongs and turned the trial against them. They could not succeed in bringing any serious and definite charges against him, even though they had the help of false witnesses; he could have mentioned certain undeniable facts, along with all the necessary details and supporting data, which would have caused the guilt of his accusers to appear in all its starkness. He could have unmasked the evil intentions and underhand tactics of these high persons, including their secret vices, and he would have caused their fine display of respectability, beneath which they were attempting to conceal their real game, to collapse like a house of cards. The trial would have resulted in the condemnation of his judges. But Christ refused to help himself by using his knowledge to overwhelm his accusers and judges. He confined himself to defending his own innocence before Annas and Caiphas and allowed the bad faith of his judges to speak for itself. He preferred to die rather than to reveal the wicked deeds of his cruel enemies.

He only uses his knowledge of other persons to the extent that he is required to do so by his love for them. When he rebukes the Pharisees because their hearts are rotten with evil thoughts which they endeavor to conceal behind a display of piety and devotion, he does so out of love for them, so that they may be forced to think of what they are doing and may finally be converted to him. When he warns Judas that he knows all about his dark projects, it is for the purpose of trying to make him give up this plotting and resume his ties of obedience. It is the equivalent of saying: "What is the good of all this, Judas? You expect to derive profit from all these schemes, but I am well aware of every one of them!" He tells the Samaritan woman exactly how many husbands she has had and that she is living with a man who is not her husband, because he wants to break down the wall of her respectability and get at the truth so that he can answer her question. His disclosure is designed to overwhelm her heart and to convert her. That is precisely what happened, for the woman realized that only the Messias could have done what he did: "Come and have sight of a man who has told me all the story of my life; can this be the Christ?" [24] Her reactions show clearly that she was not humiliated or angered by what he had told her, but that she was transformed, had had a change of heart, and was brought to believe in him because of what he had done. Christ always employed his knowledge of hearts for the improvement of mankind in order to make men respond to his love. Nothing causes us to have more confidence in someone else than the knowledge that this person knows us perfectly. Since he already has such an intimate knowledge of us, why attempt to keep anything further from him, why not abandon oneself completely to his will? Since he knows everything about our soul, why be on guard against him as we would be against a stranger; why persist in keeping from him what already belongs to him? Nathanael and the Samaritan woman were prepared to entrust themselves to one who had read their souls. This complete insight into hearts was one of the great advantages which Jesus had by virtue of his power as the Messias. It enabled his disciples to entrust their persons to the Master in complete confidence that they would be safe in his hands. They had the consolation of knowing that they were in the hands of one who knew them intimately.

The psychologist is often inclined to be merciless in his analysis. He takes a secret delight in uncovering

[24] John 4:29.

the multiplicity of selfish tendencies which influence the individual, the complexes of his unconscious self; in short, everything that makes him unattractive and disfigures him. He is expert at uncovering dishonorable motives under honorable guises, and lofty ideals are frequently treated as if they were sublimations of instinctive impulses. He distrusts the loftier expressions of the soul. He is inclined to disparage what he is studying and to despise what he discovers. The penetrating gaze of Jesus never underestimated the importance of what he discovered; he never looked at any individual with a view to discrediting and despising him. Christ has a better opinion of the human heart than most psychologists have. He is able to look into the most secret recesses of the human heart and discover all the unconscious motives which affect each individual, yet he never ceases to esteem or to love men. He of course does not countenance the evil he finds there, and human selfishness finds no support in him. He does not hesitate to say to the chief of his apostles, when the latter would turn him from the road to Calvary: "Back, Satan." [25] In saying this he probes farther than the modern psychologist would in uncovering the real basis of Peter's evil thought, namely Satan. He is thus excusing the action of Peter to a certain extent; he refrains from judging the apostle on the basis of his attitude and from identifying him with Satan, who inspired him. As a general principle he refuses to identify individuals with the

[25] Matt. 16:23.

95

evil deeds which they commit. The true Peter is the one who received the promise that he would be the head of his Church and who was divinely inspired by the heavenly Father to declare that Jesus was the Messias. The esteem in which he is held by Christ is not ruined by his various lapses and failures, his opposition to the passion and his denial. Jesus refuses to identify evil purely and simply with the one who does it even in the case of Judas; he makes every effort to turn his disciple from his obstinate intention to betray him. Just as he has confidence in a better Peter than the one who denies him, so he never ceases to appeal to a better Judas than the one who plots his betrayal. Does he not permit him to retain the common purse of the group and allow him to remain among their number until the very end? This proves that Christ never lost hope that Judas would think better of what he was doing and would succeed in freeing himself from the power of Satan.

Jesus never passed judgment during his earthly life for the purpose of condemning. He never regarded himself as a grand inquisitor but rather as the good shepherd. A judge would have regarded it as his duty to punish those who had done wrong; the good shepherd endeavors to lead the sheep back, when he finds that they have wandered. Men wished to stone the woman caught in adultery, but Jesus absolves her and tells her to sin no more. The thief who is justly condemned to be tortured on the cross is not promised punishment, but a reward in the next life. Jesus' knowledge of hearts enables him to upset human judgments and restore reputations. Simon the Pharisee thought he had detected him committing a fault: "If this man was a prophet, he would know who this woman is that is touching him, and what kind of a woman, a sinner."[26] The Pharisee thought all this very evident. Was the woman at the feet of Jesus not well known in the village, was it not apparent from her demeanor and her garments what a shameful occupation she had? But Christ was able to see farther into her soul than Simon could; he recognized in her attitude a love which proceeds not from sin, but from forgiveness and from newly found innocence. The woman had ceased to be a sinner and Jesus is more of a prophet than Simon thinks he is. In his kindness he recognizes her for what she is.

The sympathy shown by Christ in his knowledge of others is especially evident in his relations with his disciples. With them it is a knowledge resulting from the life which they lead in common, like the shepherd with his sheep. The disciples are accustomed to this daily intimacy with him and know that the Master's complete knowledge of them has joined to it the most tender love. After Peter had first begun to follow Christ, he made an attempt to withdraw at the time of the first miraculous catch of fish because of his fear: "Leave me to myself, Lord . . . I am a sinner."[27] Peter knew himself guilty of sins, sins evidently open to the mind of one who had the power to command

[26] Luke 7:39.   [27] Luke 5:8.

97

the fish of the sea. But constant companionship with Jesus, the second miraculous draught of fish, and the resurrection made Peter, now even more deeply conscious of his sins and weakness because of his denial, combine loving trust with the realization that his Master was omniscient. Indeed, Peter dared to appeal to Christ's knowledge when assuring him of his love: "Lord, thou knowest all things; thou canst tell that I love thee." [28] Indeed, this is the true object of Christ's all powerful knowledge, to recognize in men their love for him, as he was pleased to do in the case of the woman who had been a sinner and the Apostle who denied him. He probes the darkness of human souls for the sole purpose of discovering a spark of this love.

When Christ wishes to explain his intimate knowledge of those who follow him, he states that it is based on his knowledge of his Father: "My sheep are known to me and know me; just as I am known to my Father, and know him." [29] Christ's knowledge of his disciples is of the highest order possible; it is not merely a psychological insight, more penetrating and fundamental than that common to men of genius, but it belongs to a different, a higher order. This knowledge is absolutely total and essential; like the knowledge which unites Christ with the Father, it wishes to bring into being a state of mutual satisfaction and understanding in which each can abandon himself to the other. We have remarked that Jesus never read men's hearts in order to spy upon them or condemn

[28] John 21:17.   [29] John 10:14–15.

98

them; he strove to be pleasing to them by establishing a relationship of love with them. Just as the eternal Father declares that he is well pleased in his beloved Son, Christ strives to win the favor of his disciples and to form a relationship with them which is as intimate and loving as his relationship with the Father. Moreover this knowledge and this satisfaction must be shared; the sheep are asked to know the shepherd as the shepherd knows them. This is why Christ gives himself to his disciples so completely.

His own know him

While he has such complete knowledge of those who follow him, he also sees to it that they have an intimate knowledge of him. His attitude to them is not that of one who endeavors to control others by his own penetrating knowledge but carefully guards all knowledge of himself for fear that he may lose the advantage of his superiority. Quite the contrary. Jesus is completely sincere in exposing himself to their gaze. He lives with them and reveals to them his state of mind by what he says and does. He purposely wishes to conceal nothing from them and has no inner retreat to which he can retire; nothing is kept from their sight. He studiously avoids the appearance of leading two kinds of lives, one for others to see and one for himself, hidden from their view. He reveals himself just as he is, and this complete sincerity on his part is one way in which he gives himself completely to his followers. Any attempt to hide anything would amount to deceit on his part and would be inconsistent with the light which he typifies; any reservation would amount to placing a restriction on the love which he desires to be boundless. He opens his heart to men in the fullest sense of the word and imparts to them all that he knows, all that he is, and all that he possesses.

In revealing to others their secret thoughts and their hidden deeds, Christ was really revealing himself. It was quite evident to Nathanael, whose character our Lord so frankly praised, that Christ was actually revealing himself to the disciple. As soon as Christ told the Samaritan woman who she was, he revealed to her who he was. By forgiving the woman who had been a sinner, he made Simon the Pharisee understand that he was indeed a prophet. He only shows his knowledge of others when they express a desire to know him; he lets himself be recognized by them and then imparts to them his own secret. He thus establishes his love on a basis of equality; otherwise his superior knowledge might spoil the possibility of such love altogether. In revealing himself to others he gives them a claim on himself comparable to his claim on them. His disciples know him as he knows them.

He treats his disciples as friends in whom one may freely confide. "I do not speak of you any more as my servants; a servant is one who does not understand what his master is about, whereas I have made known to you all that my Father has told me; and so

I have called you my friends." [30] All the disciples are privileged to share in this friendship. Jesus has not reserved this favor for anyone in particular; his friendship is granted to all. He vigorously protests against the intimation that he keeps the best of himself for his family. He publicly declares that he wishes to be on the same kind of familiar and intimate terms with all those who are disposed to listen to his words as he is with his immediate relatives: "Who is a mother, who are brethren to me?" he asks those who come to inform him about the arrival of his family. He looks not at his family, but at his disciples and followers as he stretches out his hand and says: "Here are my mother and my brethren! If anyone does the will of my Father who is in heaven, he is my brother, and sister, and mother." [31] He is even willing to apply the term "mother," which men normally reserve for the person who brings them into the world, to all mankind. He wishes to be on as intimate and affectionate terms with all mankind as he is with his mother, and the foundation of this intimacy must be the common desire to do the will of the Father. He makes a point of communicating the most intimate secrets of his heart to all. He wishes to extend his friendship to all mankind, to incorporate mankind in his family. This astonishing universality by no means lessens the intensity of his love; the heart of Jesus is not exhausted in communicating itself to mankind. He gives himself to each one with the maximum degree of affection;

[30] John 15:15.   [31] Matt. 12:48, 49–50.

his family remains his family, but one considerably expanded, and his friends are all treated as friends, numerous though they become.

Because of the universality of his love he did not attempt to reveal himself except during his public life. During the many years spent in Nazareth he did not disclose his identity as the Messias to his own relatives and neighbors. Only Mary and Joseph, who had been divinely informed of the extraordinary nature of the child, were aware that there was something more in him, something divine. When Jesus began to make himself known to men, he wished to offer himself to all; all were to be as privileged as the members of his own family. Of course, he knew in advance that many of those to whom he would attempt to reveal himself were not disposed to receive his offer. But he wished to make it clear that he was interested in all, whoever they might be, and that he could not be held responsible if anyone rejected his offer of friendship. He is like the sower who scatters his seed among thorns, on stony ground, and along the road side, as well as on good ground. It may be objected that this amounted to throwing his friendship away, but Jesus was not afraid of squandering his riches. His generosity knew no bounds; it was the generosity of a heart which was eager to give itself to all men, even at the cost of useless effort and at the risk of encountering a humiliating rebuff.

Christ thus acts in broad daylight. Those who are dominated by personal interest or factional interest generally attempt to conceal their tactics, so as to attain the goal. He who is entirely governed by a love which he offers to all and sundry has nothing to hide and welcomes the light of day, because it enables him to give himself more openly and effectively. While the Pharisees secretly take counsel to protect their position and influence against this upstart, Jesus constantly strives to uncover their designs. At his trial he can truly say that he has always spoken publicly in the temple and taught his doctrine to all who cared to listen. He does not hesitate to proclaim that he is the Messias before those who report his words to the Pharisees, because he desires to communicate to them everything which is in his heart. When his disciples strive to dissuade him from returning to Judea, where he might be stoned, he answers that he will continue to proceed in broad daylight and that he will not play hide-and-seek with his enemies. He leaves for Bethany, where he performs his most astonishing miracle, the resurrection of Lazarus. If he had agreed to hide his movements, he would have withdrawn himself from men instead of giving himself to them; he would have remained unknown to them instead of becoming known by them.

The risk he runs in revealing himself publicly shows clearly that he does not endeavor to make his revelation for his own sake, but for the sake of others. The fact that he is inspired by love is shown by the way his revelation is made; Jesus makes himself known to mankind in actions which constitute a gift. In order to let men know that he is the light of mankind, he gives sight to the blind. In order to show the power of his grace to restore, he heals many of the sick. He shows that he has power to forgive sins by restoring freedom of movement to a lame man. He shows that he is the author of life by restoring several dead persons to life. He wishes his revelation, a gift in itself, to be made known in the form of blessings, so that men can immediately derive some tangible benefit from it.

Moreover, he immediately proceeds to share his power to do these things with his disciples. He does not make himself known for the purpose of establishing an impassable gulf between himself and men or in order to relegate them to a rôle of admiration or fear. He discloses himself so that they may share in his greatness. He who says: "I am the light of the world," [32] also tells his disciples: "You are the light of the world," [33] because the illuminating power of his truth is passed on to them. He grants his apostles the power to perform miracles. Shortly after Pentecost Peter will restore to a cripple the use of his legs. But above all he gives them the power to forgive sins, a power which shocked the Pharisees, who protested vigorously against what he had done, accusing him of usurping a divine prerogative. This action of forgiving human sins clearly shows the nature of his authority and makes it evident that the Father has indeed placed all power in his hands. Instead of keeping this supreme sign of his power to himself, he invests his disciples

[32] John 8:12.   [33] Matt. 5:14.

with this authority. He alone had the exclusive authority to tell men what the Father had told him, inas-
much as he was the only one who had ever been
intimate enough with the Father to hear his most
secret words. Yet Jesus confides these things to his
disciples and instructs them to teach all nations what
he has told them. His divine power of passing from
death to life is handed on to them in the same way
when he assigns them the task of baptizing all men in
the name of the Father, the Son, and the Holy Ghost.
When he gives thanks to the Father for the resurrection of Lazarus, which he is about to perform, he says:
"Father, . . . I thank thee for hearing my prayer. For
myself, I know that thou hearest me at all times." [34]
He grants his followers this power of obtaining everything from the Father when he assures them that
whatever they ask for in their prayers will be granted
them. They will always be heard, as he himself is
heard. Jesus wishes this communication of himself to
his disciples to be so complete that anyone who welcomes them will be welcoming him, as if he were completely in them: "He who gives you welcome, gives me
welcome too." [35] He even wishes to share with them
the most fundamental part of his nature, his quality
as the Son of God; he wishes to raise them all to the
level of his divine Sonship. With regard to the principal charge which his enemies cast in his face: "Thou,
who art a man, dost pretend to be God," Jesus
answers: "Is it not written in your law, I have said,

[34] John 11:42.   [35] Matt. 10:40.

You are gods?" [36] Those who blame him for wishing to magnify himself because of pride receive the reply that he does not wish to raise himself above others, but to raise others to his level, in accordance with the promise of Scripture that man would be granted eternal life. When he reveals himself as the Son of God, he is only acting out of love, because he wishes to make men noble by divine adoption. The most serious charge which could be brought against the heart of Christ was that he was entirely motivated by colossal selfishness. His heart provides the answer to this charge in the abundant love with which he makes himself known, solely for the purpose of giving himself. Jesus shares with all and with all alike everything he possesses; this is what justifies his revelation.

Love is what gives Christ's revelation of himself its true meaning. He is not concerned to show himself for the purpose of making an impression on men or in order to gain an ascendancy over them; he is concerned with communicating himself entirely to others. Christ derives no benefit from this himself, for he has no need of anybody's approval or admiration in order to be fully what he is; it is for the benefit of men that he does this, so that they may be enriched by all that he reveals to them. Christ's revelation is not a kind of spectacle at which his disciples are privileged to be present; it is a transformation which is effected in their souls by means of all that he communicates to them. Those who share in the knowledge of himself

[36] John 10:33, 34.

106

which Jesus offers, agree to bind themselves to him with ties of love, receive the complete gift of his person, and be entirely changed and renewed by his gift. The revelation of Jesus has an effect on men, because they are the object of his love.

Sharing in common

That this revelation was accomplished by the sharing of his whole nature and his whole heart with others, the Gospel allows us to gather from the fact that his public life was passed in the midst of a group of disciples. The Gospel does not pretend to give us all the details about this life for the simple reason that a life shared with others is bound to include many things which are relatively unimportant. It can only mention some of his more important actions which impressed his disciples: actions which reveal his gratitude to the Father, his mercy, his anger, his sorrow, his goodness and his admiration. It should be emphasized that Jesus does not conceal his emotions even when they are humiliating and likely to discredit him. Men are usually moved by pride to conceal their feelings of fear or sorrow; but Christ allows Peter, James, and John to behold his feelings as the passion draws nigh: his sudden fear, his weariness, his distress, the gloom and sadness which overwhelm his soul. "And now he grew bewildered and dismayed: My soul, he said to them, is ready to die with sorrow." [37] Christ allows all to see how he fears the pain which he is

[37] Mark 14:33-34.

to suffer. He holds tenaciously to the principle that his heart is to be an open book for his disciples. Previously he had revealed his joy to them, desiring that they share it, especially the joy he felt when giving thanks to the Father. In the talk after the Last Supper he had even dared reveal to them the joy he felt in returning to the Father; he willed to associate them in his joy because of his genuine love for them. In like manner he endeavors to have his apostles share in his sadness during the agony.

During this great moment of his life he shares with them all that he feels and does. He wishes his suffering on Calvary, the supreme revelation of his love, to be shared with his disciples. On the road to Golgotha he shares with Simon of Cyrene the weight of the cross. This is symbolic. For some time he had been warning those who would follow him that they must be prepared to take up their crosses. "Have you strength to drink of the cup I am to drink of?" [38] he asked James and John. Shortly before his passion he told his disciples that the tragedy which was soon to occur would be only the beginning of an entire series of trials which would afflict them: "All this is but the beginning of travail. But you will have to think of yourselves; men will be giving you up to the courts of justice, and scourging you in the synagogues, yes, and you will be brought before governors and kings on my account, so that you can bear witness to them." [39] Christ's own tragic appearance before the Sanhedrin,

[38] Matt. 20:22. [39] Mark 13:8-9.

his trial before Pilate, the governor of Judea, and his scourging will not be experienced by him alone. He desires to share these experiences with others. He does not pretend to reserve a superior part for himself in all this, a part from which others must be excluded; he does not will to save men all by himself, rejecting their cooperation. He wishes the chief act of the work of redemption, this amazing act which is destined to prove his love for men through suffering, to be accomplished with the help of all. That is why he suffers the torments of crucifixion in the company of a few faithful followers—above all, his mother—who share in the drama they are obliged to witness. We are not told to take up our crosses merely to do penance; Christ offers us this opportunity to share in his passion and to follow his example because of his love. This is not a demand motivated by revenge, but a desire inspired by love. Is it not a fact that Christ associates with himself in his suffering those whom he loves most? Mary is the one who stands closest to him at the foot of the cross; and his favorite disciples, Peter, James, and John, are those who remain with him to watch and pray the night of his arrest. To the disciples who fail him at this time he will furnish other occasions to prove their love. To Peter, who confessed his love and was given supreme power over the Church, Christ promises a death like his own: "When thou hast grown old, another shall gird thee, and carry thee where thou goest, not of thy own will." [40] The magnificent and

[40] John 21:18.

generous appeal he will make to Paul through the disciple Ananias also includes a promise of the same sort: "I have yet to tell him, how much suffering he will have to undergo for my sake." [41] Paul rejoices and glories in being able to relive the death of Christ: "With Christ I hang upon the cross." [42] The cross is Christ's most precious gift, a gift which he grants generously to those whom he loves the most. It sums up the essence of his life and is the symbol of his affection for men; by sharing it with them he grants them the best part of himself.

Nothing is omitted in the communal life which Christ leads with his disciples. He gives them his whole person and, above all, what is closest and dearest to his own heart. He wishes no limits to be placed upon his generosity, which will endure even after he has gone: "And behold I am with you all through the days that are coming, until the consummation of the world." [43] He refuses to take back what he has once given. He will continue to share with his disciples his life, his person, his thoughts, his powers, and his divine mission, as he did during the course of his earthly life.

THE GOOD MASTER

Understanding the mystery

It is obvious from his teaching that Christ really intends to make a complete gift of himself to his dis-

[41] Acts 9:16.

[42] Gal. 2:19.

[43] Matt. 28:20.

ciples. He transmits to them all that he has learned from the Father. "And he said to them, It is granted to you to understand the secret of God's kingdom." [44] Even mysteries are revealed to the apostles. In the apocalyptic literature of the time the term "mysteries" was applied to teachings which were generally not revealed to the uninitiated and were concerned with the last things. Christ reveals to his apostles God's secret purpose to grant salvation to mankind, the intention which he had kept in his heart for so many ages and had now determined to reveal in his person. His disciples are thus informed about God's wonderful plan and are able to penetrate his secret thoughts. The mystery of Christ is not something which is destined to remain hidden from men or to be only partially revealed to them because of its transcendent nature and their inability to grasp it. Jesus is not satisfied to open the door half-way, he opens it all the way, he "gives" them the mystery. His mystery, of course, surpasses the capacity of the apostles to understand it; but what "flesh and blood" cannot understand, the illumination of the heavenly Father will make clear. Hence Christ does not hesitate to reveal to his disciples the essence of the divine wisdom, that "depth in God's nature" [45] which the eye of man cannot see nor his ears hear nor his spirit penetrate, but which the Spirit knows thoroughly and will help them to understand. This willingness of Jesus to impart his knowledge is in marked contrast with the attitude of

[44] Mark 4:11.　　　　[45] I Cor. 2:10.

111

many wise men and religious thinkers in antiquity, who were willing to communicate their "mysteries" only to a small circle of initiated persons. They regarded their knowledge as a secret possession which must not be indiscriminately divulged because it formed the basis of their superiority over other men and was a source of profit to them to the extent that they could exploit it for their own advantage. As opposed to this jealous attitude on their part, Christ is prepared to communicate the mystery of his doctrine to all. He does not disdain to reveal his sublime message to crude fishermen of Galilee, who have had no training in the knowledge of the law. He imparts a knowledge of the most transcendent truths to them. It is a mark of the Master's essential goodness that he teaches them all that he knows.

This is the way he behaves towards his disciples, but perhaps he adopts another attitude towards the crowds. Does he not observe greater reserve with them? "It is granted to you to understand the secret of God's kingdom; for those others, who stand without, all is parable: so they must watch and watch, yet never see, must listen and listen, yet never understand, not ever turn back, and have their sins forgiven them." [46] Those standing without are the crowd massed around the house where Jesus is talking with his disciples; the crowd cannot enter the house and by the same token cannot understand the mystery of his teaching. Certain commentators have drawn from this

[46] Mark 4:11–12.

passage the conclusion that Jesus employs parables for the purpose of hiding the meaning of his teaching from the crowd; some have even maintained that he does this for the purpose of bringing about his own death. But this would amount to attributing an evil intention and diabolical scheme to Christ. Can we seriously believe that his parables, charming and simple stories in themselves, were invented for the purpose of misleading his hearers? Could the one who took pity on the crowd because it had no shepherd have wished to be a false shepherd to them, a robber who would lead them astray? The Gospel is full of instances of Jesus' love for the crowd; he is continually speaking to them; he shows concern for their misery and works many cures among them. He proclaims the blessedness of the poor, the oppressed, and the unfortunate who follow him. Jesus is entirely sympathetic to the crowd and the crowd returns this sympathy. It follows close at his heels and endeavors to find him when he withdraws into the wilderness. It is very fond of his sermons and listens to them for hours on end; it signifies its admiration for the miracles he performs and its enthusiasm is so great it would proclaim him king of Israel. In fact, it is so attached to the Master that the Pharisees are afraid of its reaction when they decide to get rid of Jesus; they are obliged to proceed with caution so as not to wound the sensibilities of the people. The crowd acclaims Christ as he makes his triumphal entry into Jerusalem shortly before his passion. Jesus could not have been prejudiced in any way against the crowd; and the crowd, if left to its own devices, would not have shown any hostility to him. The Master would have failed in his high mission if he had used parables for the purpose of concealing his teaching from the crowd which loved him so much.

Hence St. Mark does not have the Lord say: "I speak to them in parables so that they may *not* see and *not* understand," but: "For the others, who stand without, all is parable: so they must watch and watch, yet never see. . . ." The fact that the crowd must be content with parables is not a situation which he particularly likes. Quite the opposite. It is the result of an existing state of affairs which he can only deplore. He regrets that the crowd must be content with parables and that he is powerless to explain the true meaning of his teaching to them. He would like to raise their minds to a more serious understanding of his message, but is prevented from doing so by the propaganda of the Pharisees. Their ill will is the reason why the crowd must be content to "watch and watch, yet never see." The Sower's enemy, Satan, is the one using the Pharisees to prevent the seed from being sown in their hearts. His adversary resorts to all kinds of tricks so that the majority of Christ's hearers will have to be content with parables; while they look at him and listen to him, they can neither see him nor understand him and are thus kept from being saved. Parables are intended to serve as an introduction to the light of his kingdom. By means of them he hopes to appeal to the rough intelligence of the crowd and make them understand as much of his doctrine as they can grasp. His parables are not intended to conceal his teaching or to serve as a kind of half-truth, but are intended to acquaint the crowd with as much of his revelation as they can comprehend. St. Mark clearly states this when he says: "And he used many parables of this kind, such as they could listen to easily, in preaching the word to them." [47] They could not understand any more, partly because of their limited intelligence, and partly because of the propaganda carried on among them by the Pharisees. Christ, however, allows no obstacle to stand in the way of his revelation; he reveals to all as much as they are capable of understanding, whether it be the crowd or his own disciples. Parables are the way in which he expresses his love for the common people, a love which does not refuse to use the humblest kind of means to bring them knowledge of the most sublime truths.

Even in the case of his own disciples Jesus feels that he is unable to tell them everything in view of their inability to understand. "I have still much to say to you, but it is beyond your reach as yet. It will be for him, the truth-giving Spirit, when he comes, to guide you into all truth." [48] The only limitation accepted by Christ in imparting his doctrine is the one imposed upon him by the actual inability of his apostles to understand. But this is only a temporary restriction. Jesus is firmly resolved to reveal everything; those things which they have not been able to learn from

[47] Mark 4:33.   [48] John 16:12–13.

his own lips will be learned from the Spirit, who will be sent to them for this purpose. Christ is determined to impart to his followers absolutely all that he knows.

He causes the blind to see

The task is difficult, but he sets about it with tireless energy. How often is he obliged to tell his disciples that the kingdom he has come to found is not a kingdom of this world, yet shortly before his ascension they again put the same question to him: "Lord, dost thou mean to restore the dominion to Israel here and now?" [49] His disciples are stubborn to the very end in their inability to grasp the spiritual meaning of his doctrine. Another person would have been irritated by this continual failure to understand; but Jesus prefers to interpret their question not as a political one, but in a spiritual sense as a reference to the true kingdom of God. He answers that the various phases in the establishment of this kingdom will be determined solely by the will of God and that it is not for his disciples to know what they are. He adds that their task will be to spread the kingdom by bearing witness to it in the farthest corners of the earth. Having enlightened his disciples so many times about all this, he still has the patience to answer a question which shows a complete lack of understanding on their part of the spiritual nature of his message and is kind enough not only to repeat what he has so often said before but to shed further light on the whole matter. The same is

[49] Acts 1:6.

116

true of his teaching about the passion and the resurrection. He prophesies on several occasions that he will be tortured and put to death and that on the third day he will rise again from the dead. He even foretells some of the things which will occur during his passion: "Now, we are going up to Jerusalem; and there the Son of Man will be given up into the hands of the chief priests and scribes, who will condemn him to death; and these will give him up into the hands of the Gentiles, who will mock him, and spit upon him, and scourge him, and kill him; but on the third day he will rise again." [50] But even this precise display of knowledge on his part is not enough to convince them. James and John ask him again for the privilege of being seated at his right hand and at his left hand when he comes into his glory. After his resurrection he will again speak about this matter, which he had attempted to explain so many times before, when he shows the disciples on the road to Emmaus that the Messias is destined to undergo suffering and so enter into his glory. "Too slow of wit, too dull of heart!" [51] he says to Cleophas and his companion, as their hearts burn with the hopeful and encouraging things he tells them along the way. He could have been extremely irritated with their attitude on this occasion, but he only takes them to task in a gentle sort of way for the purpose of rousing them from their lethargy. He explains the Scriptures to them at great length and accepts their failure to understand as an excuse for

[50] Mark 10:33-34. [51] Luke 24:25.

explaining the meaning of his teaching with greater determination and clarity than ever before. His attitude towards them is similar to his attitude towards sinners. He approaches them with greater love the more miserable they are because of their sins. Whenever he encounters an obstinate spirit in his hearers, he is driven to enlighten and to convince them with greater zeal than ever. The good Master has a generous heart like the good shepherd and desires above all to help those who tend to elude him.

If he strives to enlighten his apostles when he finds that they are having difficulty in understanding his doctrine, he is even more intent on preaching to the people, when he finds that they have been worked upon by the Pharisees and show signs of turning away from him. This is the moment he chooses to perform the greatest miracle of his public life, the resurrection of a man who had been dead for four days. The resurrection of Lazarus is a good example of a parable which actually takes place before the eyes of the people and is, therefore, more impressive than any second-hand report. The crowd is always impressed by vivid imagery, but in this case Jesus furnishes them with something better than imagery; he performs an act which shows unquestionably that he is capable of conquering death and restoring to life. This impressive demonstration of his power produces such an effect on the crowd that the Pharisees complain to one another: "Do you see how vain are your efforts? Look, the whole world has turned aside to follow after him." [52] The crowd which saw him raise Lazarus from the dead is the same one which will acclaim him at Jerusalem. At the very moment when the crowd appears about to abandon him, he speaks to them with more compelling authority than ever before and practically shouts his message to them, as if he wished to be understood by a man who had stuffed his ears. In spite of the danger threatening him he speaks out louder than ever before in one last attempt to make them listen to the truth. It is part of the logic of his love to expend itself more generously the greater the obstacles which he encounters.

He enlightens his enemies

This desire to enlighten minds as much as possible, especially those deliberately closed to him, is characteristic of the way he treats his enemies, as we can see on almost every page of the Gospel. The Sadducees question him about fine points of the Law in order to cast ridicule on his doctrine: "We had seven brothers once in our country, of whom the first died, a married man without issue, bequeathing his wife to the second. And the same befell the second brother, and then the third, and in the end all seven, the woman dying last of all. And now, when the dead rise again, which of the seven will be her husband, since she was wife to them all?" [53] It is obvious from the nature of their question that the Sadducees are not

[52] John 12:19.   [53] Matt. 22:25–28.

interested in seeking his advice; they simply wish to embarrass him. In spite of their evil intention, Jesus undertakes to enlighten them and in doing so teach them something as well, the reality and purity of life in the next world: "When the dead rise again, there is no marrying and giving in marriage; they are as the angels in heaven are." [54] The Pharisees are far more assiduous in plying him with double-edged questions. In order to "put him to the test," [55] they ask Jesus whether it is lawful for a man to put away his wife. Jesus seizes the opportunity to explain to them the whole divine plan with regard to the indissolubility of marriage. Others ask him for a sign from heaven when they see him performing so many miracles; instead of pointing to the evidence of these miracles as an appropriate answer to their question he says: "The generation that asks for a sign is a wicked and unfaithful generation; the only sign that will be given it is the sign of the prophet Jonas." [56] He thus foretells his own death and resurrection, the essence of the drama of redemption. While his enemies attempt to catch him in error, he unveils before their eyes the fundamental mystery of the kingdom of God. The doctor who tries to engage him in a rabbinical discussion by asking what is the greatest commandment of the Law receives the answer that all man's moral acts can be summed up in two commandments. To those who question him with a view to opposing his revelation

[54] Matt. 22:30.   [56] Matt. 12:39.
[55] Mark 10:2.

and disregarding his teaching he fully and skillfully explains the true meaning of his doctrine. They attempt to ensnare him in the darkness of their ignorance; he bathes them in his light. They try to trip him up on the ever dangerous rock of politics: "Master, we know well that thou art sincere, and teachest in all sincerity the way of God; that thou holdest no one in awe, making no distinction between man and man; tell us, then, is it right to pay tribute to Caesar, or not?" How full of flattery and insincerity their words must have sounded! Christ trembles with indignation at their deceit and upbraids them for their hypocrisy: "Hypocrites . . . why do you thus put me to the test?" But instead of giving way to this indignation and brushing their question aside he undertakes to answer it and, in doing so, formulates a principle which is destined to be of supreme importance in the relations between Church and State: "Why then, give back to Caesar what is Caesar's, and to God, what is God's." [57] These few words suffice to solve a problem which had been raised solely to embarrass him; he insists on edifying those who wished to ensnare him.

Even when he appears to avoid answering a question, because of the obvious insincerity of those who ask it, he is at pains to point out the general outline of his reply. While he is teaching in the temple, the chief priests and the elders of the people ask him: "What is the authority by which thou doest these things?" Jesus asks them a question in turn: "Whence

[57] Matt. 22:16–17, 19, 21.

did John's baptism come, from heaven or from men?" When they hesitate to answer, Christ says to them: "And you will not learn from me what is the authority by which I do these things." [58] His refusal to answer actually amounts to an answer for those who are able to understand what he means; Jesus is saying that he is acting by virtue of the same authority to which John appealed, the authority of God.

Christ continues to proclaim the kingdom of God in spite of his enemies' attempts to involve him in disputes and catch him in their subtle toils. He continues to proclaim the kingdom to the end. When the last trap is laid and Caiphas solemnly adjures him to declare whether he is the Son of God, he makes a final attempt to enlighten his enemies by proclaiming the supreme truth of his whole life. He continues to be the good Master towards the spiteful Pharisees even to the end. Although he had ample reason to break with them and could easily have punished them by his silence, he never gave up the attempt to enlighten them. He generously responds to all their questions, questions designed to bring about his death.

A doctrine which appeals to the freedom of love

It is remarkable that this extreme generosity is accompanied by profound respect for human freedom. Christ never allows himself to be carried away by a wild zeal that would have done violence to consciences. He could easily have dazzled men by his

[58] Matt. 21:23, 25, 27.

genius, conquered them, and forced them to do his will; but he steadfastly refrains from doing so, because he wishes to develop, rather than to subject, the souls of those who are attracted by his love. He has no desire to add anything to the existing code of Jewish law; he undertakes to free his disciples from the complicated mass of rules and regulations with which the Pharisees had surrounded the Law, charging the latter with a much too literal interpretation of the laws governing the observance of the Sabbath and the various fasts. He is opposed to all those who would impose upon the people further demands which they themselves are unwilling to bear. He adopts a way of life which is in evident contrast with that of John the Baptist; the latter was noted for his extreme self-mortification, while Jesus openly dines and sits at the table with anyone who happens to invite him or receive him. He eats and drinks, and he does this as a matter of course. His first concern is that his disciples should feel joy in their hearts like the joy which the bridegroom feels at the wedding feast. Joy of this kind could not have been felt, had he been given to austere practices of self-mortification. He, of course, had no need to ward off the divine anger through the exercise of various privations. He wishes to show that he is grateful for God's goodness in causing his Son to live among men. This extraordinary favor merits rejoicing. Christ endeavors to broaden souls and open up hearts.

He teaches with authority, and his hearers are conscious of the difference between his methods and those of the scribes, who constantly appeal to the authority of a text. Christ achieves this superior authority not by overwhelming consciences by what he has to say, but by favoring their spontaneous development. He declares that he is master of the Sabbath and exempts his followers from the dead weight of the many traditional observances. In his sermon on the Mount he shows that he is the founder of a new morality: "It was said to the men of old. . . . But I tell you. . . ." [59] All the precepts of his teaching are designed to break through the shell of outer observance for the purpose of developing a fuller appreciation of spiritual values. He wishes to free his disciples from the vain casuistry of oaths and to promote the simple use of yes or no. He advises them to pray in secret, to avoid the use of complicated phrases, and to address themselves to God in complete sincerity. He changes the order of penalties which had been fixed by the Pharisees for offenses against one's neighbor in assigning the most severe penalty for the least offense. He endeavors to show that external actions are less important than internal dispositions; the smallest ground for complaint should be settled before anyone goes to make an offering to God. In the same way he minimizes the importance of rules concerned merely with external purity, such as washing before meals and avoiding all contact with sinners, and insists upon the importance of purity of heart. He defines sin, not with reference to a violation of the rules governing the use

[59] Matt. 5:21, 22.

of various foods, but with reference to evil thoughts, which are nourished in the soul. By freeing consciences from a system of practices which tend to suffocate them, Christ wishes to assist men to realize their good intentions. He gives a stricter interpretation to marriage by forbidding divorce and by condemning those who even look at anyone with the intention of committing adultery as guilty of adultery. He refuses to place any restrictions on the love of neighbor, a love which must be observed even towards enemies, and we must never refuse to forgive. He would do away with the usual excuse for a misunderstanding, namely, that the other is responsible: "If thou art bringing thy gift, then, before the altar, and rememberest there that thy brother has some ground of complaint against thee, leave thy gift lying there before the altar, and go home; be reconciled with thy brother first." [60] He expressly refers to the case in which "thy brother has some ground of complaint against thee," rather than to the case in which "thou has some complaint against thy brother," to indicate that there is no excuse for ill will or unwillingness to forgive; everything must be done to settle differences, even when one's neighbor is clearly in the wrong or is motivated by ill will.

This shows us what Christ means when he says that he has come not to set aside the Law, but to fulfill it. He has come to promote a better observance of the spirit of the Law, which has been neglected. When he asks his disciples to show more justice than the

[60] Matt. 5:23–24.

scribes and Pharisees do, he is not demanding that they should observe more practices than they, but that they should live up to those they observe better than others do. When he says that the smallest detail and the smallest jot of the Law shall not disappear, he does not mean to imply that they must observe all the formalistic regulations of the Law, for he is the first to disregard them himself. What he means is that his disciples should not be limited in their observance of the spirit of the Law; there must be no compromise, for example, when it comes to love of neighbor.

Christ is an exacting Master in this respect; but it is obvious that this strictness is motivated by his goodness, for it aims to make men observe the spirit of the law of their own accord. He completely upsets the accepted notion of the way to fulfill the Law and gives a new meaning to the Law itself. He declares that love is the sum of all the commandments. For a Law which was concerned with exacting obedience and imposing burdensome observances he substitutes a simple precept, which by its very nature is capable of being fulfilled in a completely non-compulsory and voluntary way and in a spirit of self-sacrifice. He prescribes the goal toward which men are expected to strive in such a way that the desire to attain this goal seems to spring from the innermost depths of their being; each one is allowed to achieve this goal through sacrifice in the way that is best suited to his personality. Christ wishes to deliver men from the great fear which threatens them, because he loves them; he even dares to base the entire structure he intends to build on love and requires that love shall carry out the divine will. He tells his disciples time and time again that they must obey his commandments, but this obligation is always presented as an invitation of love. "If you have any love for me, you must keep the commandments which I give you"; "The man who loves me is the man who keeps the commandments he has from me"; "If a man has any love for me, he will be true to my word"; "the man who has no love for me, lets my sayings pass by." [61] These are the terms he uses when he prescribes his law to the disciples. We have only to recall the mighty display of power which accompanied the granting of the Law to Moses and the terror which the Israelites felt on that occasion, if we wish to get an idea of the difference which separates the two laws. Christ does not count on terror for the enforcement of his law but on the attraction of his person. He has sufficient confidence in men to offer them a way of life in which the necessity for law is accompanied and modified by the spontaneousness of love.

When he wishes to present them with a picture of true perfection, he does not list the various articles of a code of law, but gives them a collection of beatitudes. "Blessed are the poor in spirit . . . the patient . . . the clean of heart . . . the merciful . . . the peace-makers . . . those who hunger . . . those who mourn . . . and those who are persecuted. . . ." [62]

[61] John 14:15, 21, 23, 24.　　　[62] Matt. 5:3 ff.

Christ proclaims the ideal he has come to preach under the positive form of blessedness; he minimizes gloomy thoughts of restraint so as to arouse a joyous response among his hearers. He is not content to urge those who are suffering to be resigned; he promises that their affliction will be turned into joy. By offering men a moral doctrine in which the cross plays such an important part, he shows them that he is with them, not against them; that he desires their happiness and will furnish them with the most appropriate means of achieving it; that in his person the supreme power of God, while remaining wholly transcendent, is pleased to reveal itself in the form of goodness and accept as its goal the greatest possible happiness for mankind.

A light which does not blind

Christ shows the same respect for individuals in the way he wins people to his cause. He could have revealed himself in such a compelling way that all would have been obliged to believe in him, but that would have amounted to forcing souls to believe and getting possession of them in spite of themselves. He prefers to proclaim his message and present himself in a much more modest light, which is sufficient to stimulate belief, but not so blinding or dazzling as to sweep away all opposition. He does not even try to impose himself on his disciples; he leaves them the possibility of abandoning him, if they choose. Yet the ties of friendship which bind him to them are very strong. When his talk on the Eucharist turned a great

128

many away and he is inwardly distressed, he asks his disciples: "Would you, too, go away?" [63] Jesus hopes with all his heart that they will react as Peter will on another occasion; the great affection which he has always felt for his disciples is greatly increased on this occasion when so many appear to have left him; his heart would break were they also to go away. Nevertheless, in spite of his great hope and love, he will leave the choice of staying or leaving entirely up to them. He has no wish to monopolize those who follow him and compel them to come after him against their will. This would amount to loving them not for themselves, but for his own sake. He wishes his disciples to give free expression of their attachment to his own person and to nourish that attachment on love; consequently he leaves the matter up to them. If they are of the opinion that they cannot endure to hear what he has just said about giving his body to eat and his blood to drink, then it is better for them to go their way. It is up to them to decide.

He is careful to bring no pressure to bear on their minds, as he could have done, for example, if he had kept repeating that he was the Messias and drilling this into them until they had no choice in the matter but to believe. Instead, he calls himself by the mysterious title "Son of Man" and allows his apostles to gather that he is the Messias from the miracles which he performs. When John the Baptist sends legates to find out whether he is the one who is to come, Jesus

[63] John 6:68.

answers by pointing to the miracles he has performed: "The blind see, and the lame walk, and the lepers are made clean, and the deaf hear . . . the dead are raised to life, and the poor have the gospel preached to them." [64] It is up to John to draw his own conclusion. It is likewise up to the apostles to discover the Messias in Jesus and to proclaim him as such. "Who do men say that I am?" Various opinions are being circulated on this score; some think that he is John the Baptist, others Elias or one of the prophets. The reason for this is that Christ has not yet declared specifically that he is the Messias. "Then he said to them, And what of you? Who do you say that I am?" Peter is the first to recognize him as the Messias: "Thou art the Christ." [65] This confession of faith on Peter's part is truly a discovery; he is not repeating a lesson he has already learned, but is announcing a discovery he has just made of his own accord, inspired by the Father. Christ is not a Master who speaks for his pupils; he develops their awareness of the supernatural to the point where they can perceive the truth for themselves and reach a solution of the problem of his person, aided and guided by his grace.

The best indication that he gives men complete freedom in this respect is provided by the fact that a certain number resisted him. The Pharisees called him a seducer and perverter of souls and would never allow themselves to believe in him, yet Christ never appealed to the need for saving them from the terrible

[64] Luke 7:22.   [65] Mark 8:27, 29, 30.

consequences of their obstinacy as an excuse for doing violence to their souls or trying to win them over in spite of themselves. Judas continues to belong to the number of the twelve and will remain with them until the end. Jesus does everything he can to regain his affection through gentleness and by refusing to bring any pressure to bear on him, although he certainly had the means of imposing his will, had he so desired; the love of Judas is what he desires and nothing else.

Let us return for a moment to the story of Christ and the rich young man. The young man, greatly enthusiastic about Jesus, is moved to approach him, and the Gospel tells us that he runs towards the Master, kneels down before him, and makes a request which indicates that he has completely opened his soul to him: "What must I do?" [66] Will Christ take advantage of his enthusiasm and use this as a means of persuading the young man to follow him? Not at all. He tries first to calm him and to make him reflect. He wants him to regain his poise. He deliberately cools his emotion by telling him that he is mistaken in calling him "Good Master," because only God is good. Then, in order to give him time to collect himself, he goes through the list of the commandments, although he is aware from the first that the young man expects to hear something more from him than that. When the latter tells him that he has observed all the Law, Christ "fastened his eyes on him, and conceived a love for him." [67] How deeply this look of love must have

[66] Mark 10:17.   [67] Mark 10:21.

131

penetrated the young man's soul and how strongly he must have felt the pull of Christ's love! Yet this look would not compel him to love in spite of himself, for the young man's face falls when he hears what Christ would have him do and he goes away. Christ refuses to violate his freedom of choice in spite of the great love which he feels for him. He shows that he is truly the Good Master by refusing to take a soul which the young man was only willing to offer him on the spur of the moment.

When he later overturns Saul on the road to Damascus in an extraordinary scene, which befits this extraordinary person, he does not deprive him of his basic freedom by this blow. This is proved by the fact that Saul has sufficient strength of mind to ask him several questions. He submits to Christ of his own accord: "What must I do, Lord?" [68] Jesus has no wish to exploit the complete power he has gained over Saul; he must rise and take the time to recover from his shock; at Damascus he will be told what to do. Christ specifies what he is to do, but he does not compel the zealous Pharisee to follow him; he safeguards his right to make up his own mind. Paul will have his chance to make his act of faith, after he has reflected on what has occurred and is in full possession of all his faculties. In recounting his experience later to King Agrippa Paul adds that he was not disobedient to the heavenly vision; he could have refused to believe, but he chose to submit in accordance with the dictate of

[68] Acts 22:10.

his conscience. Christ did not win the soul of his former persecutor by stunning him; he freed him from
the weight of the past and from his Jewish prejudices
so that he could pronounce for or against with a completely open mind. Freedom was not taken from Paul
on the road to Damascus; it was given to him.

This concern of Christ to preserve the freedom
of others shows how sincere his love really is. The
most powerful personality history has ever known
never attempts to dominate the personalities of those
whom he seeks to attract, because he desires to help
them and to awaken their souls. As the light of mankind, he has no desire to be surrounded by shadows.
He is responsible for the amazingly rich development
of the personalities of Peter and Paul. As the Good
Master he assumes full responsibility for their education and imparts to them the great richness of his
message and his life; but he leaves them the freedom
of their souls, because they are far too dear to him ever
to be subjected to any kind of violence or constraint.

THE FRIEND

The Friend

Christ came into the world to win men's devotion and to draw all mankind and the world to himself. But before he asks for this devotion, and in order
to obtain it, he first attaches himself to men. His goodness is primary and prevenient. He therefore makes no
attempt to appear as a conqueror who has come to

establish his power, or as a propagandist who tries to impose his ideas by making a great deal of noise. Christ is fundamentally inspired by a desire to win souls to his cause, and he will even employ moments of rest for the purpose of spreading the Gospel, as in the case of the Samaritan woman. But before he takes anything from anyone, he wishes to give something; by giving himself, he invites the gifts of others. God though he is, he entrusts himself to the tender care of Mary and Joseph and thus wins their hearts. The first two disciples who ask where he lives are invited to follow him; he offers them himself along with the hospitality of his house. Before accepting Peter as a fisher of men, he does him a good turn by granting him a plentiful catch of fish. When the Samaritan woman comes to the well, he will reveal himself to her by asking for a drink. He is the one who seeks out the publicans and sinners, and he gives himself to them by showing obvious sympathy for them. He delights in their company and in the free exchanges which take place between guests at their meals. He even consents to take part in such exchanges with the Pharisees by accepting their invitations to dine. The same practice is followed with those who accompany him from place to place, his disciples and the small group of faithful women. This giving of himself sums up the story of his appearance on earth, from the moment of his Incarnation when he abandons himself to the womb of a woman until his final passion when he abandons himself to the hostile kiss of Judas, the troop of soldiers who come to arrest him, the Sanhedrin, Pilate, and the cross.

This giving of himself results in the formation of many strong friendships with all that that word connotes in the way of affection. Christ, above all, gives his heart, and it is the heart of others which he wishes to receive. He describes himself as a bridegroom at a wedding-feast, as one moved by the tenderest feeling of love, yearning to share with those around him the full measure of his joy. His disciples are not asked to observe fasts and other forms of penance, because he wishes to celebrate this love with them in all its splendor. He places affective love before effective love, which consists in the performance of works. In the house at Bethany Martha becomes distraught while preparing the meal and feels that she is being neglected; she wishes Mary to lend her a helping hand instead of sitting at the Master's feet. Christ, however, shows greater appreciation for the affectionate devotion of Mary than he does for the hustling of Martha and tells her so. "Only one thing is necessary," [69] to give our hearts to him. We must always begin with effective love, for that is what gives merit to what we do. The example of Martha shows that it is possible to withhold a part of one's love from Christ while attempting to serve him. Jesus had no greater enemies than those who pretended to serve God by performing all the prescriptions of the Law, while failing to love him sincerely. The "best part" chosen by Mary as she

[69] Luke 10:42.

sits at the feet of the Master listening to what he has to say and completely devoted to him is precisely what Christ wishes to offer men, when he approaches them as if he were going to a wedding-feast. It is the part of a fervent and deep love.

The well-beloved disciple

Christ's friendship assumes different forms. His love for Peter and for John appears to have been outstanding in the case of his disciples, but he loved them in different ways. His love for John is more tender, and John will be known as "the disciple whom Jesus loved." All the disciples were, of course, "disciples whom Jesus loved," but the words indicate that he had a particularly tender love for John, a love corresponding to John's sensitive nature. John is attracted by Christ from the first moment he meets him. Until then, apparently, he had been a follower of John the Baptist in his search for an ideal way of life and a spiritual master. It is not difficult to understand that the gentle ways of Jesus must have made an immediate impression on him, compared with the harsh asceticism of the Baptist. He therefore abandons the company of the austere prophet who threatens the people with divine wrath to follow the "lamb of God," who has come to take away the sins of the world. He feels a special need for affection himself and is drawn to a Master whose preaching is so obviously inspired by his pity for the crowds and whose miraculous cures show that he is constantly moved by goodness. Hence he is the disciple who becomes the closest follower of Jesus, in the sense that he is the nearest to him and most sensitive to all the manifestations of his friendship. Along with Peter and James he witnesses the Transfiguration on Thabor and the agony in the garden at Gethsemani. But above all he has the good fortune to lie on Christ's breast at the Last Supper. The physical heart of Jesus has a particular meaning for him, and he abandons himself to it, so to speak. This action marks the climax of his friendship and expresses the full measure of his love; it is also destined to remain the permanent symbol of this love, for John will be called the "disciple who leaned upon the breast of the Lord." At Calvary John takes his place at the foot of the cross along with the women, and Christ confides to him the one he holds dearest in this world, his own mother. He gives the most loving of his disciples his most tender gift. The friendship which John had formed with the Son was destined to be continued with his mother in the same atmosphere of gentle affection. At Calvary John also witnesses something destined to make a profound impression upon him, the piercing of the side of Jesus by the spear of the soldier. The spear of course only pierces a dead body, but it reaches the human heart on which the beloved apostle had been leaning less than twenty-four hours before in a transport of love. In the same way that the gift of his heart on the previous evening had been a symbol of his great friendship for him, so the piercing of his side now appears to John as a symbol of a love which has suffered to the bitter end. This spectacle serves to bind him to Christ more closely than ever and puts the seal, as it were, on their friendship.

John is the first of the apostles to arrive at the empty tomb on the morning of Easter. He is also the first one to recognize the Lord on the shore of the sea of Tiberias, because his love is more tender and therefore more perceptive. Finally, Christ promises John that his death shall be a prolongation of their friendship. The chief of the apostles is destined to undergo martyrdom, but John will only have to remain here until the Lord comes. His death will recall their intimacy at the Supper; Christ will simply come and allow the apostle's head to rest on his breast. The beautiful expression often used to describe a Christian death, "going to sleep in the Lord," is especially applicable in the case of John, because he learned so well to know the meaning of that rest.

Peter

His friendship with Peter is of an entirely different sort, rough and ready. John was attracted by the personality of Jesus as soon as he heard him preach; his words and his kindly face were enough to convince him of the rest. Simon is much more practical and less contemplative; he is more impressed by deeds. Jesus therefore does something to win his adherence. "When he had finished speaking, he said to Simon, Stand out into the deep water, and let down your nets for a catch." This was bold advice for an amateur to give to a professional like Simon. Jesus interferes in Simon's field, because he wishes to found his friendship with him on a bold stroke. The boldness of the stroke both surprises and intrigues Simon. His reaction is typical of the way he will frequently behave on such occasions; he first draws back and then throws himself into the venture with greater energy than ever. His first reaction is one of amazement at the apparent absurdity of the demand of Jesus: "Master, we have toiled all the night and caught nothing"; but he immediately adds: "at thy word I will let down the net." After considering the objections for a moment, he throws himself into the task whole-heartedly. The words of Christ produce what a whole night of labor had not been able to achieve, a remarkable catch of fish. Simon's reaction to this miracle is characteristic. He falls down and catches Jesus by the knees: "Leave me to myself, Lord, he said, I am a sinner." Christ calms him and says reassuringly: "Do not be afraid; henceforth thou shalt be a fisher of men." [70] Simon was drawn to him with greater love than ever, though first he desired to leave him because of his unworthiness. This is precisely the way Christ wished it to be; he wished to win him over by a bold stroke.

We have just observed that Peter's reactions are apt to be very positive one way or another; he is inclined to devote himself whole-heartedly to whatever he is doing. The knocks and the blows will certainly not be spared him, but these collisions and signs

[70] Luke 5:4–10.

of weakness will serve to stir up his devotion and make him more attached to Jesus than ever. Christ is fully aware of this whole-hearted spirit of his, and that is why he employs boldness in his case; he will not hesitate to require a great deal from him. But first he gives, and the generosity which he displays will be far greater than that of his apostle. St. John tells us that, when they first met, Jesus gave Simon a new name: "Thou art Simon, the son of Jona; thou shalt be called Cephas, (which means the same as Peter)." [71] At the very beginning of their friendship Christ, in an abrupt way which suits the temperament of the apostle, presents him with the gift of a marvelous future which his new name is meant to symbolize. Simon is destined to become the foundation stone of the Church. The generosity of the miraculous catch of fish foreshadows the generosity of Simon's new name as Peter; the quantity of the fish typifies the great number of souls he is destined to win for Christ.

The friendship of Christ and Peter continues, as it began, with evidence of great generosity on the part of the Master and expressions of faith on the part of the disciple. When Jesus approaches the boat of the apostles at night by walking on the water, he terrifies them so much that they cry out for fear. Peter is terrified along with the rest, but in accordance with his usual habit shows as much confidence as he had fear, as soon as he hears the reassuring voice of the Master. "Lord, if it is thyself, bid me come to thee

[71] John 1:42.

over the water." This is the way Christ hoped that he would react; he wishes to associate Peter with this manifestation of his power and so bids him come to him over the water. So Peter ventures down from the ship and boldly walks on the top of the waves towards him. The friendship of Christ and his disciple is symbolized by this attempt to approach each other in defiance of the elements. By sharing with Peter his miraculous power to walk on water Jesus affords the disciple a glimpse of the power of his Church, which will be miraculously preserved against all the storms of the future. But, when Peter notices the force of the wind, he begins to lose faith and to sink into the waves, whereupon he cries out louder than ever: "Lord, save me." Once again momentary weakness causes him to appeal for help and Jesus reaches out his hand to save him. "Why didst thou hesitate, man of little faith?" [72] Although greater than that of the other disciples, his faith is still too weak; Jesus expects more from Peter, his best friend. The boldness of his faith must be boundless.

After his sermon on the Eucharist, Jesus asks the apostles: "Would you too go away?" He was probably looking straight at Peter as he said this. The Master would suffer terrible agony were the twelve also to abandon him, and the distress which he feels inwardly is matched by the visible distress of Peter, who cannot tolerate the idea of deserting him: "Lord, to whom should we go? Thy words are the words of eternal

[72] Matt. 14:28–31.

life." [73] The attempt of Jesus to gather his disciples about him at this critical moment brings forth an expression of Peter's faith in him in the face of possible desertion by the others. Their lives are so bound together that any separation at this point would amount to a real tragedy for both. "You, too," Jesus says to the disciples, as he asks them whether he is about to lose everything that is dearest to his heart. "To whom should we go?" Peter asks, as though the thought of being separated from the Master had suddenly made him feel faint. The souls of the others echo the same thought.

The friendship of Peter and the Master strongly and profoundly affects both. When the Master asks him: "And what of you? Who do you say that I am?" Peter's answer shows his realization of Jesus' true nature: "Thou art the Christ, the Son of the living God." [74] In perceiving the secret of his personality Peter has gone farther than the others; he discloses on this occasion something which Jesus himself will only reveal at his trial before Caiphas. The boldness of Peter's faith is thereupon matched by the boldness of the Master's promise. Peter declares that Jesus is the Messias, and Jesus announces that the disciple is destined to be the head of his Church. The Master penetrates deeply into the soul of the apostle when he declares: "And I tell thee this in my turn, that thou art Peter and it is upon this rock that I will build my

[73] John 6:68–69.   [74] Matt. 16:15–16.

church. . . ." [75] They are henceforth bound together
in friendship by the greatness of their common
destiny, by a profound understanding of one another,
and by a mutual confidence which nothing can ever
shake.

Their friendship will shortly be tested by a great
crisis, which will serve to strengthen this bond. Peter
and our Lord have entirely different concepts regarding the rôle of the Messias. Peter dreams of a glorious
Messias, whereas Jesus knows that he is destined to
undergo suffering and death. When he foretells his
death, Peter draws him aside and remonstrates with
him: "Never Lord, he said; no such thing shall befall
thee." Christ's reaction is instantaneous: "Back,
Satan; thou art a stone in my path; for these thoughts
of thine are man's, not God's." [76] He promptly rebukes his disciple, because he is sure of the great
strength of their friendship; he feels the seductive
power of the tempter all the more, because it is re-
layed to him through the mouth of the apostle whom
he dearly loves. The suggestion is more dangerous than
his temptation in the desert: then he had faced Satan,
his implacable foe; now it is his true friend who is
tempting him with love and in a voice which he delights to hear. Jesus is obliged to defend himself
against his own heart; he does not wish to be influenced by Peter and so protests violently against his
suggestion, behind which he can easily discern the evil
presence of Satan. By giving way to a perfectly natural

[75] Matt. 16:18.   [76] Matt. 16:22–23.

feeling, suggested by the spirit of evil, Peter was attempting to block the path of the Master and would have caused him to fall. The tenderness of Christ's heart is evident even in the midst of his indignation; his reaction discloses the great influence which the wishes of his friend can have over him.

This incident occurs shortly before the Last Supper. When Peter beholds Jesus gird himself with a towel and wash the feet of the disciples, he is filled with indignation. He cannot tolerate the idea of the Master stooping to fulfill the rôle of a servant. When Jesus comes to him, he can stand it no longer and says: "Lord, is it for thee to wash my feet?" It is of no avail for Jesus to say to him: "It is not for thee to know, now, what I am doing; but thou wilt understand it afterwards." Peter refuses to be mollified: "I will never let thee wash my feet!" Finally, Jesus argues: "If I do not wash thee, it means thou hast no companionship with me." Simon must make up his mind, either to let Christ do it or to lose his friendship forever. When confronted by this last terrible alternative, his love surges up stronger than ever and he completely gives in. This is the way he usually acts; after a moment of hesitation, he gives in completely. "Then Lord, said Peter, wash my hands and my head too, not only my feet." [77]

These collisions are destined to prepare him for the great test of Christ's passion, which will shake his friendship to its very foundations. Jesus warns him of

[77] John 13:6–9.

the temptation which threatens him; Satan will attempt to sift him like wheat. But he assures him that he has prayed for him, so that his faith will not fail. Even though Christ is abandoned by all at the hour of his danger, he will not be one to abandon his own friends. Just as he once reached out a hand to save Peter when he began to sink in the waves, so he will agree to take him back again, as soon as he shows that he is sorry for having denied him. Christ will even dare to say to him: "When, after a while, thou hast come back to me, it is for thee to be the support of thy brethren." [78] Despite his denial, Peter will be called upon to support the others and he will succeed in doing so, not by virtue of his own strength, so piteously weak, but with the help of the Lord.

Peter will not believe Christ when he clearly tells him that he is destined to deny him thrice. It would be hard to believe that anyone with such a noble spirit could do such a thing in any case. "Lord, said he, I am ready to bear thee company, though it were to prison or to death." [79] When Jesus is arrested, Peter has hardly shaken off his drowsiness before he is ready, sword in hand, to defend his Master and prepared to die, if need be, to save him. The only trouble with this display of bravery is that it is entirely natural, far too natural. Peter's confidence in his own strength is far too great. He has not yet fully understood that friendship with Christ can only exist on a supernatural basis. It is true that he has been bound to the Master

[78] Luke 22:32.   [79] Luke 22:33.

thus far by the supernatural inspiration of his faith, the revelation of the Father, which enabled him to realize that Jesus is the Messias, and by his complete confidence in the power of Christ, which permitted him to walk on water. He must now look at the passion from the same supernatural point of view, if he is to understand and to accept it. The passion is meaningless, even repugnant, from the natural point of view. Because Peter failed to watch and to pray with him in the garden at Gethsemani, he now appears before the soldiers with a purely natural courage. Christ condemns his resort to violence and heals the wounded servant.

With that, the courage of the apostle collapses and he flees with the others. When he returns to the place where the trial is taking place, he is so dominated by fear that he denies three times, in the presence of servants and by-standers, that he knows the accused. It is at this point that Jesus renews his ties of friendship with him. Just as Peter is denying him the third time, the cock crows, "And the Lord turned, and looked at Peter." [80] This look saves him; Jesus is not condemning him, but reminds him of his love. Peter thereupon goes out and weeps over a fault he knows is already forgiven.

After his resurrection Christ makes it clear to Peter that his privileged position as head of the apostles is unchanged; Peter is the first of the apostles to whom he appears. The intimate bonds between

[80] Luke 22:61.

146

Peter and Christ are sealed forever at this meeting on the shores of the sea of Tiberias. The circumstances are the same as on the occasion when Simon left all to follow the Master. It is as if he were being called a second time. All night long they have labored and caught nothing. "Cast to the right of the boat and you will have a catch." [81] For the last time Christ wishes Simon to understand that, when human efforts fail, confidence in the Lord will produce amazing results. The miraculous catch of fish on this occasion symbolizes what he is prepared to do. After they have eaten together, Christ says to Peter: "Simon, son of John, dost thou care for me more than these others?" His question is intended to show the great importance he attaches to his love for Peter; he insists upon a direct answer. "Yes, Lord . . . thou knowest well that I love thee." Christ thereupon matches this declaration of love with a corresponding favor, when he makes his disciple the pastor of his Church: "Feed my lambs." Jesus then asks Peter the same question a second time and receives a similar answer. The third time his voice is characterized by greater tenderness than ever, and he uses the more affectionate word, "love." Recollection of Peter's denial inspires him to make this third and final bid for the apostle's love. A feeling of sadness comes over Peter as he replies more firmly than ever: "Lord, thou knowest all things; thou canst tell that I love thee." Jesus thereupon confers on him again his function as head of his Church and predicts the form

[81] John 21:6.

147

of his martyrdom: "Believe me when I tell thee this; as a young man, thou wouldst gird thyself and walk where thou hadst the will to go, but when thou hast grown old, another shall gird thee, and carry thee where thou goest, not of thy own will." [82] Such is the culmination of their friendship. Christ hands on to Peter his own function as good shepherd and transmits to him at the same time the prerogative of a shepherd: to lay down his life for his sheep. This will be the final test of their friendship. Peter is finally bound to experience himself the same fate he was so anxious to spare the Messias at Calvary.

This completes the transformation of Simon into Peter. By adapting itself to the blunt and vigorous personality of Simon the friendship of Christ is able to bring about a complete change of heart in him. It takes over all his valuable natural characteristics, but completely changes them in the process. Peter is so convinced of his own strength that he must be shown that he is in reality very weak and that true strength can only come from the Lord. In order to win the soul of Peter, Christ allows him to labor all night without catching any fish, to sink in the water, and to deny his Master. In return, he asks him to have faith in a power capable of providing him with a miraculous catch, supporting him on the water, and arousing an even deeper love in him after his shameful fall. We have seen how Jesus takes advantage of Peter's natural inclination to throw himself into anything with renewed

[82] John 21:15–18.

energy after an initial phase of hesitation to make the disciple learn to distrust himself and to rely entirely on the support of the Master. Simon is thus transformed into the unshakable rock on which the structure of Christ's Church is destined to be built. Even his denial does not result in the withdrawal of the privileges which have been extended to him; on the contrary he is definitely confirmed in them once and for all. His denial is used by Christ as an excuse for giving the apostle greater authority by way of erasing the memory of his past offense. Christ constantly endeavors to use such occasions in order to show how generous he can be towards his friends. Simon's consciousness of his own guilt fortunately predisposes him to realize that he really owes everything to someone else and must depend upon him for support. This brings about in him a complete change of a supernatural character. The friendship of Christ is grace which transforms and changes the soul of Peter; it is also grace which is not discouraged by his momentary lapses; and finally, it is grace which combines tenderness with strength and founds the most daring of all enterprises on the gift of a heart: "Dost thou love me?"

Lazarus

His friendship with Lazarus is of another sort; it is a friendship which affords him relief and relaxation from the cares of his ministry. The Gospels tell us very little about this peaceful and apparently little known

149

friendship. When St. Luke describes the scene at Bethany involving Martha and Mary, he makes no mention of Lazarus. We are allowed to assume that Jesus was fond of passing through Bethany, because he could find relief from the strain of preaching at the house of his friend, Lazarus, in the easy give-and-take of familiar conversation, which was no doubt characteristic of this household, and also because he was sure of finding there unfailing loyalty and a retreat from the hatred which pursued him on all sides. When Lazarus becomes ill, his sisters let Jesus know by sending the simple message: "Lord, he whom thou lovest lies here sick." [83] There is no need to mention his name; Lazarus is the one the Lord loves.

Christ does not immediately set out for Bethany, but sends a reassuring message instead: "The end of this sickness is not death; it is meant for God's honour, to bring honour to the Son of God." [84] The meaning of the message is not entirely clear, but there seems to be reassurance in the words: "The end of this sickness is not death." In any case this promise sufficed to maintain their courage; Jesus would certainly not abandon his friend. Christ's fidelity to his friend, however, will demand considerable courage, for Jesus is aware that he will be exposing himself to attack by his bitterest enemies if he tries to pass through Judea and will, in fact, be risking his life. "Master, his disciples said to him, the Jews were but now threatening

[83] John 11:3.   [84] John 11:4.

to stone thee; art thou for Judaea again?" [85] When the Master insists on going, they are under the impression that they are all going to their deaths. "Thereupon Thomas, who is also called Didymus, said to his fellow-disciples, Let us go too, and be killed along with him." [86] Jesus is prepared to make every sacrifice for the sake of going to the help of Lazarus; he wishes to be faithful even to the point of death, and neither the threats of the Pharisees nor the objections of his disciples can keep him from going to a friend who has need of him.

He shows on this occasion that his friendship is not only fearless but also characterized by tenderness and affection. His words to the apostles clearly indicate that he is moved by a feeling of love: "Our friend Lazarus is at rest now; I am going there to awaken him." [87] He speaks as if he considered Lazarus merely asleep, that all he had to do was to go and awaken him, and that he continued to observe the same familiarity with him in death as he had in life. It is possible to suppose that Jesus felt no regret for his death in view of his power and intention to restore him to life. He even speaks joyously of the great surprise he has in store for them before leaving for Judea: "Lazarus is dead. And for your sakes, I am glad I was not there; it will help you to believe." [88] Yet, when he reaches Bethany and sees Mary fall at his feet in tears and the weeping of the others who accompany her, he is

[85] John 11:8.
[86] John 11:16.
[87] John 11:11.
[88] John 11:15.

greatly affected. He is hardly able to ask: "Where have you buried him?" before he breaks down. "Jesus wept. See, said the Jews, how he loved him." [89] The fact that Jesus weeps for his dear friend, as he is about to grant him the joy of being raised from the dead, shows that he wishes to feel all the emotions of love, even those which he might logically have spared himself. Is it not characteristic of love to be easily moved by the emotions and for the heart to be influenced by sympathy? In this connection there is obviously a great difference between the ideal behavior of Jesus and the attitude of the Stoics, who tried to suppress their emotions. The Gospel tells us expressly that Jesus "sighed deeply." The Stoics believed that emotion was a sign of weakness and failed to understand that true love accepts this weakness and interprets it as a sign of dependence on the person who is loved. The tears of Christ are a sign of weakness and those who witness this scene are not wrong in interpreting this as a sign of his great love for Lazarus.

When he reaches the tomb, he is again greatly affected by his grief. He feels the sadness which men normally feel before the tomb of a recently departed friend or relative. Then he regains his usual composure and orders the stone to be taken away; after calling on the Father, he causes the dead man to emerge from the sepulcher. The Gospels give us no details about what he actually said to his friend Lazarus on this occasion, but the emphasis placed upon his sorrow

[89] John 11:34, 35–36.

would appear to indicate that he was glad and expressed his joy at seeing him return to life. He who had wept but a few minutes before for his departed friend no doubt shed tears of joy when he had found him again.

This important event links the friendship of Jesus and Lazarus with the drama of the redemption. We have already seen how his friendship with Peter brought about in the latter a change of a supernatural character. We might have expected that his friendship with Lazarus would remain completely calm and outside the work of redemption, so to speak, since Lazarus was not one of the twelve and there was no intention to make him an apostle. But Christ is determined to act boldly in his case also, for he allows his friend to die and exacts the supreme sacrifice from him. In other words, he upsets the normal course of his friendship with Lazarus and incorporates it in the supernatural plan of redemption by causing Lazarus to die and to be raised from the dead as a prediction of his own death and resurrection. Jesus desires the fate of his friend to be a prediction of his own fate. This terrible, and at the same time most noble, gift of his love is the greatest favor he can confer on him.

Judas

We come now to the saddest part of the Gospel, Christ's friendship for Judas, a friendship painful and rejected. No other friendship shows so clearly that Jesus loves before being loved, and even without being loved. When he summons Judas to follow him, he surrounds him with all the love and hope he has for the others and shares with him all that he gives the others: the joy of being closely associated with him, the secrets of his teaching, and the intimate thoughts of his heart. He chooses him to be one of the pillars of his Church and destines him to sit on one of the twelve thrones that have been prepared for the judgment of Israel. He sends him to spread the good news with the seventy-two disciples and causes him to perform wonders. But the time comes when Jesus wishes to raise his friendship for the apostles to a higher level. He is not content with the purely natural enthusiasm which they show when he performs the miracle of multiplying the loaves of bread. In his sermon on the Bread of Life he endeavors to explain the spiritual meaning of this miracle by promising to give them his body to eat and his blood to drink. Only one answer is possible after this mysterious discourse, which turns many of his hearers away: faith. All the apostles express their faith in the Master except Judas. He abandons him in his heart, but determines to stay with him for reasons of self-interest. Christ, of course, tries to make it perfectly clear that he is not deceived by the disciple's false attitude: "One of you is a devil." [90] He is content to let the hint drop. He could have driven Judas away indignantly, but prefers to keep him among the group in the hope of his eventual conversion. In other words, Judas is allowed to remain one

[90] John 6:71.

of his friends; and his hypocritical attitude, which must have greatly offended Jesus, is not allowed to interfere with this friendship. He persists in loving one who henceforth can think of him only in terms of the profit he can derive from him; while Judas strives to bring about his ruin, Christ endeavors to exert his love for the purpose of winning back this corrupted disciple and saving him from the consequences of the crime he is about to commit.

Christ henceforth is conscious that someone is spying upon him, exploiting him, intent on selling him at a convenient opportunity. When Mary Magdalen pours expensive spikenard ointment over his feet at Bethany, Judas blames him for allowing her to be so extravagant: "Why should not this ointment have been sold? It would have fetched two hundred silver pieces, and alms might have been given to the poor?" [91] Christ is apparently not worth two hundred pieces of silver himself, for Judas has already bargained with the chief priests and is ready to settle for much less. The action of Mary makes him realize that the price he hopes to get from the Pharisees, two dozen pieces of silver, is a ridiculous figure for Christ and that he is being cheated in his contract with them. Perhaps this is the reason why he protests so loudly against her action. In any case Christ simply answers all these insulting calculations of his by approving the act of Mary without attempting to reveal the hidden motive of his disciple.

[91] John 12:5.

Jesus makes a last attempt to turn Judas from his purpose at the Last Supper. He first lets them all notice his sadness: "Jesus bore witness to the distress he felt in his heart." Then he declares something which completely astounded them and which they could hardly believe: "Believe me . . . believe me, one of you is to betray me." [92] He attempts to soften the hardened heart of Judas by his display of sorrow and appeals to his intelligence to make him realize that none of his schemes has escaped the knowledge of the Master and that it would therefore be much better for him if he simply gave himself up. Christ has refrained so far from mentioning Judas by name, whenever he alluded to the fact that one of the twelve was about to betray him. He thus gave him the opportunity of changing his mind without letting the others know that he had ever entertained any disloyal thoughts. In spite of his several warnings the disciples are still at a loss to know who is meant and discuss the matter among themselves. At this point Jesus resolves to play his last card, but shows all the tactfulness of a friend in doing so. In order to make a suitable impression on Judas, he reveals to John that the traitor is the one to whom he will hand a piece of bread; whereupon he hands the piece of bread to Judas. This action of handing him the bread is his way of offering to renew their friendship, if Judas had so desired, and is tantamount to saying: "Judas, I know perfectly well that you are a traitor and can name you as such at this

[92] John 13:21.

156

moment. But I am ready to take you back as a friend, if you will change your attitude." Judas maintains his obstinate and deceitful attitude, for he accepts the piece of bread, but refuses to change his attitude. Hence the Evangelist declares: "The morsel once given, Satan entered into him." [93] Satan had, of course, taken up his abode in him long ago; but each time he rebuffed the love of Christ, Satan entered deeper into his soul. Having failed to win him back through kindness, Jesus now attempts to threaten the traitor with the dire consequences of what he is about to do, in order to make him give up his intention. "The Son of Man goes on his way, as the scripture foretells of him; but woe upon that man by whom the Son of Man is to be betrayed; better for that man if he had never been born." [94] This is not a final condemnation, but a terrible threat calculated to make the traitor reflect on what he is doing. As Judas slips out of the room and disappears in the night, Jesus still tries to make an impression on him: "Be quick on thy errand!" [95] He would pursue his friend even in the midst of his bitter disappointment.

Even when Judas comes with the guard to seize him, Jesus will attempt to win back his traitorous heart. As the traitor comes up to him and kisses him, Christ warns him in the same way he did when he handed him the piece of bread: "My friend, on what errand hast thou come?" [96] He allows himself to be

[93] John 13:27.
[94] Matt. 26:24.
[95] John 13:27.
[96] Matt. 26:50.

157

embraced in the consciousness of his own sincere love and in the hope of winning him back, although all is deceit and calculation on the part of Judas. He then reveals to him his sorrow, his perfect knowledge of everything, his abhorrence of the infamous deed, and his feeling of love, which is still capable of forgiveness, as he complains: "Judas, wouldst thou betray the Son of Man with a kiss?" [97] Who knows whether Jesus may have later caught his eye for a brief moment in the course of his trial, as he did in the case of Peter, and tried again to win him back?

Christ remained the friend of Judas to the very end, but he could not prevent this friendship from being turned into a tragedy. Judas became more and more opposed to him, because he refused to recognize the supernatural nature of their friendship. Peter ceased to have confidence in his own strength and by placing all his faith in Christ set the example for all the other apostles. Lazarus was willing to die for the sake of being born again; and all the other friends of Christ were obliged to lose themselves, in order to be found again. But Judas had no intention of submitting to this condition and wished to retain complete confidence in the good things of this world. When he finally understood the ridiculous value of the price he had received for his act of betrayal, instead of attempting to renew his confidence in Christ, he gave himself up to the despair of those who are conscious of the harm they have done and the vanity of earthly things.

[97] Luke 22:48.

He ruthlessly cut himself off from all attempts to save him exerted by a friend who never abandoned him until his final gasp, although Judas had long since ruined all the good he had been able to bring about in him. Christ was loyal in his friendship to the very end and asked the Father's forgiveness for Judas, along with the others; but by hanging himself the traitor seems to have gone as far as he could to reject the noble offer of love.

The unknown disciples

We have mentioned some of the details about Christ's friendships with certain individuals to illustrate the way in which he was bound to each one of his disciples. The Gospels only mention some of the more salient features about these various friendships as they have a bearing on the life and teachings of Christ, whose explanation is the main purpose of the Gospels. One incident, however, has been preserved which sheds considerable light on the way in which Jesus is careful to maintain these personal ties even with those disciples who appear to be lost in the great number and who are not otherwise mentioned in the Gospels. This concerns his appearance to the two disciples on the road to Emmaus after his resurrection. These disciples do not belong to the group of twelve apostles, yet in the excitement of the first day of his resurrection he does not overlook them.

They are leaving Jerusalem, because they have been disappointed in their hopes with regard to the

Master. While walking along they are suddenly joined by a stranger. Christ takes particular delight in coming to the assistance of his disciples at critical moments. On this occasion he first expresses a kindly interest in them: "What talk is this you exchange between you as you go along sad-faced?" [98] Then he invites them to give the reason for their sadness, knowing what a relief it is for anyone who is suffering to be able to explain the reason for his distress. This whole exchange is not a mere game as far as Christ is concerned. Jesus knows what his disciples will say to him and how he can cure their sadness, but he desires first to sympathize with his friends and share their misfortunes, so that he can assist them to overcome them. Paradoxical as it may seem, we now find one who has just risen from the grave, joyous and triumphant because of his recent victory over death, sharing the sadness of those still mourning his death and refusing to believe the rumors of his resurrection. Every sign of human misery still strikes a sympathetic note in his heart.

After listening to them for a few moments Jesus startles them, rousing them from their sadness and encouraging a note of optimism. "Too slow of wit," he says to them. He then proceeds, by recounting the history of the prophets and by explaining to them how the Messias is destined to enter into his glory through suffering, to show them how blind they have been. The disciples are apparently not at all offended by the

[98] Luke 24:17.

160

way in which this stranger chides them for their ignorance and explains the Scriptures; rather, they are delighted to hear what they, in their heart of hearts, had always hoped might be the case, that their sadness was without foundation and that they have not correctly interpreted the events of the past few days. He thus helps them regain their confidence. As a matter of fact, they are so intent on what he is saying that, when they come to the village and Jesus indicates his intention to go on, they beg him to remain with them. This again is not a mere gesture on the part of Christ; he pretends to go on so that he might arouse a reaction in them. He is fond of acting this way with his friends in order to draw them out. Thus far he has imposed upon them as a stranger, but now that they are beginning to see the light and to recognize him, it is up to them to decide whether the conversation is to be continued. The prospect of losing someone who has just succeeded in lifting their morale to such an extent produces the desired result. What pleasure it must have afforded him to hear them say: "Stay with us!" [99] They allege the lateness of the day as an excuse, but all three know that this is only an excuse. Christ came into the world so that men could attach themselves to him, so that they could force him to stay with them. He thus achieved all that any friend could have desired.

The story ends with a meal which friends cus-

[99] Luke 24:29.

tomarily share in common. Christ had already shared so many meals with his disciples that it was easy for them to recognize him, as soon as he broke bread. As soon as their eyes were opened, he disappeared from their midst. But he left them the warmth of his presence, which they had felt on the road: "Were not our hearts burning within us when he spoke to us on the road . . . ?" [100] This warmth immediately filled them with such enthusiasm that they hastened to return to Jerusalem and tell the others.

This friendship is a typical example of all the others which Christ formed with his faithful followers. He walks with them along the road and makes a point of joining them at the moment when their hearts seem overwhelmed with sadness. Then he gradually transforms their sadness into joy by reminding them of the fundamental doctrine that salvation has been achieved through passion and that happiness can only be attained through suffering. He inspires his disciples with such an enthusiasm for his person and his presence that they force him to remain with them. Still he always remains more or less unknown to them, like a bashful friend who is intent on escaping when he has been caught and disappears when he seems to have been recognized. He remains near at hand at all times and is both visible and invisible. By insinuating himself into the silent conversation of souls, he succeeds in transforming monotonous and lonely lives by the warmth of his friendship.

[100] Luke 24:32.

The women

The Gospels inform us that men were not the only ones who were privileged to enjoy his friendship; he shared this privilege with women also. According to St. Luke, he is followed by a certain number of women as well as by the disciples: ". . . he went on journeying from one city or village to another, preaching and spreading the good news of God's kingdom. With him were the twelve apostles, and certain women, whom he had freed from evil spirits and from sicknesses, Mary who is called Magdalen, who had had seven devils cast out of her, and Joanna, the wife of Chusa, Herod's steward, and Susanna, and many others, who ministered to him with the means they had." [101] These women are part of his following, just as the disciples are, but they are not being trained or instructed in the same way and are not destined to fulfill the same functions. They perform various tasks connected with the maintenance of the apostolic brotherhood. If they are less concerned with listening to the teaching of the Master, they are more closely devoted to his person and are more loyal to him during his passion. They do not hesitate to follow him to Calvary and take up their stand at the foot of his cross. They embalm his body before it is laid in the tomb and are the first to arrive at the tomb on the morning of the resurrection, because of their great desire to be with the Master again, even if it can only be with his dead body. They feel unable to get along without

[101] Luke 8:1–3.

Jesus. When Mary Magdalen sees the empty tomb, her reaction is just what we might have expected it would be. The disappearance of his body is not nearly such a great catastrophe as his death on the cross, but Mary bursts into tears, as if he had been taken from her the second time. "They have carried away my Lord . . . and I cannot tell where they have taken him." Jesus is her Lord and belongs to her just as much as she belongs to him. In her distraction she turns to someone whom she takes to be the gardener: "If it is thou, Sir, that has carried him off, tell me where thou hast put him, and I will take him away." [102] This is a foolish thing for her to say, for whoever had taken the body would certainly not be willing to give it up, and Mary could not have carried it herself in any case. But so anxious is she to find Christ again that nothing seems impossible to her. This shows how complete her devotion to Christ is. Jesus rewards her loyalty and firm desire to find him again by revealing himself in a most touching way and by yielding to her expression of joy. He purposely appears to the women who followed him before disclosing his resurrection to the disciples.

Christ rewards Mary on this occasion for her persistent effort to find him, but it is usually the other way around; he is the one who shows the initiative in seeking friends. St. Luke recalls the way in which some of these friendships were formed. In general it can be said, on the basis of information furnished by the

[102] John 20:13, 15.

Gospels, that Jesus is very sympathetic towards women, including those who are not models of virtue. In this connection it is sufficient to recall his attitude towards the woman caught in adultery, the repentant sinner who came to the house of Simon the Pharisee, the Samaritan woman, the Chanaanite woman, and the widow of Naim. He sometimes shows considerable boldness in addressing women in public; his apostles are shocked when they find him conversing with the Samaritan woman at Jacob's well. But these contacts are always inspired by the purest kind of love and there is never any doubt about his feelings of kindness for those who have sinned; no one questions the spotless purity of his heart. The Pharisees constantly spy on everything he does, but they never cast suspicion on him in this regard. The intimate friendship of Jesus with the women who follow him is on a higher plane, where there can be no question of suspicions of this sort. Like the rest of Christ's friendships these too are destined to lead to the supernatural and involve the participants in the purifying drama of redemption. The greater the love of these women for Jesus, the more they are affected by his passion, and the harder it is for them to bear being separated from him in death. Their friendship subjects them to a terrible ordeal, which purifies their human hearts and prepares them for the divine joy of the resurrection.

Jesus maintains a firm friendship with Lazarus apart from the rest of his disciples and a similar kind of friendship with his two sisters, Martha and Mary, apart from the rest of the women who follow him. "Jesus loved Martha, and her sister, and Lazarus." [103] During his visits with them he is happy when Mary comes and sits at his feet to listen to what he has to say or just to be near him and enjoy his presence. He defends her against the charges of her sister Martha and says that she has chosen the better part. He is very grateful for the devotion of Mary when, shortly before his passion, she comes to pour a pound of spikenard ointment over his feet, because he realizes that the great value of the ointment is an indication of the great affection she has for him. Again he defends her against the charges made against her; what she has just now done out of pious devotion, other women will soon do for him: "She has anointed my body beforehand to prepare it for burial." Jesus makes it perfectly clear that he approves her action by saying: "I promise you, in whatever part of the world this gospel is preached, the story of what she has done shall be told in its place, to preserve her memory." [104] Her action was humble and simple, and Christ feels that the love which inspired it is worth remembering. He rewards the devotion and generosity which inspired her by proclaiming the nobility of what she has done to the farthest corners of the earth.

Martha and Mary are not among the women who accompany Jesus to the cross. While they are thus spared the full horror of witnessing his crucifixion, they are by no means exempted from the general law

[103] John 11:5. [104] Mark 14:8–9.

of his friendship; they too must undergo an ordeal if they are to have a share in the work of redemption. Lazarus is therefore allowed to die, in spite of their hope that he might be saved. We can readily imagine from what they both said to him on this occasion: "If thou hadst been here, my brother would not have died," [105] that the attitude of Jesus was completely dumfounding to them and that their love for him must have suffered a cruel blow. Nevertheless their faith persists and will eventually be rewarded. Christ is at pains to show them that it is not hard-heartedness on his part which prevented him from coming to the help of Lazarus, for when he sees them in tears he too is affected and weeps along with them. The sorrow which he inflicts on those whom he loves causes him to suffer also; and this mutual suffering, which is invariably followed by mutual joy, serves to put the final seal on their friendship.

Paul

The friendship of Jesus and Paul is of a different sort, for it is no longer friendship with "Christ in the flesh," but with Christ in the spirit. Nevertheless, it has many characteristics in common with his other friendships mentioned in the Gospels. It also involves a complete change of heart, which occurs in a dramatic way on the road to Damascus and continues throughout his life. Paul is obliged to give up his Jewish past, his fondest beliefs, his dearest affections; and he must

[105] John 11:21–32.

undertake the conversion of the Gentiles, although he had always been so attached to his own people. Like Peter, he is forcibly made to realize the weakness of mere human strength and of his own character, powerful though it is; he is brought to place all his confidence in the strength of Christ. He receives a "thorn in the flesh," which continually reminds him of his own weakness. When he asks the Lord to deliver him from this affliction, which seems to be an obstacle to his missionary work, he is told that he should rejoice in his infirmity, because this makes it possible for Christ to act more effectively in him. With this thought in mind, Paul refers several times to his former rôle as a persecutor; the things he did then are an indication that he has become what he is by virtue of grace, by means of the strength of Christ, and not through any merit of his own. Just as supreme power was conferred upon Peter after he had denied Christ, so the powers of an apostle are given to Paul after the persecution which he had instigated against the Church.

Paul realizes quite well that this complete change, a change affecting his whole being, is Christ's way of associating him with his passion, and he sees this as a sign of his love. His trials do not turn him from Christ, but serve to unite him with Christ. "Who will separate us from the love of Christ? Will affliction, or distress, or persecution, or hunger, or nakedness, or peril, or the sword? For thy sake, says the scripture, we face death at every moment, reckoned no better than sheep marked down for the slaughter. Yet in all this we are conquerors, through him who has granted us his love." [106] Paul realizes that his own personal experience is a constant reminder of the death of Jesus and of his passage from burial to a life of glory. He lives in association with the suffering and risen Christ. Does he not have a greater feeling for his passion than those disciples who formerly deserted the Master when he was being arrested? In the case of Paul this friendship has much more of a spiritual meaning; it is truly a life "in Christ."

Paul has the feeling that he is encompassed on all sides by the love of Jesus: "With us, Christ's love is a compelling motive," he wrote to the Corinthians.[107] The intensity of his love recalls the mysterious sensation which burned the hearts of the disciples on the road to Emmaus; just as this feeling forced them to set out immediately for Jerusalem to inform the others, so it caused Paul to travel far and wide in his missionary work. According to Paul the love of Christ surpasses all understanding; this again reminds us of the experience of the disciples at Emmaus, whose eyes were unable to recognize Jesus. Christ is both visible and invisible; in order to become aware of him and his friendship, we must be able to recognize the supernatural.

Finally, Paul has a great longing to escape from this earthly kind of association, in which Christ is continually eluding him at the same time that he is con-

[106] Rom. 8:35–37.   [107] II Cor. 5:14.

tinually giving himself to him, and exchange this imperfect state for the perfect state of his friendship: "I long to have done with it, and be with Christ." [108] "To be with Christ" is the perfect way to summarize everything that friendship with Christ means to him.

Friendships which save

Christ's friendships with John, Peter, Lazarus, Judas, the disciples, Mary Magdalen, Martha and Mary, the women, and Paul, all have certain peculiar characteristics which are in keeping with the individual dispositions of these friends; but they also have certain broad traits in common. Christ makes it clear in all cases that his love is a tender affection springing from the heart and appealing to the heart; at the same time his love is something vigorous and bold which stuns the soul. Each one of these friendships is integrated into the plan of redemption and raised to a supernatural level. By associating his friends with the drama of his passion he endeavors to show them that they must lose themselves if they would achieve salvation, and that the failure of man makes possible the triumph of God. Strong personalities like Peter and Paul, by being made aware of their own faults and failings, are forced to admit their own weakness as human beings and place all their confidence in Christ. Judas alone of the twelve refuses to make this renunciation of earthly values and abandon himself to the Savior; as a result, the tireless love of Jesus can achieve noth-

[108] Phil. 1:23.

ing in his case. Christ makes this fundamental demand
of his friends, because he loves them not superficially,
but completely and profoundly and desires to make
his love effective in them by transforming them completely. His friendship aims at winning the whole person in order to raise him to a higher level; it gains a
foothold through gentleness, but then spreads out
once it is inside with a remarkable force which
amounts to a revolution in the spiritual life of the
individual. It consumes everything in the process of
forming a new life.

THE SAVIOR

His goodness

We do not propose to consider here the way in
which Christ achieved salvation for mankind, but
what induced him to assume his rôle as the Savior.
The main consideration which moved him was made
clear both in private conversation with various individuals and in his public sermons: "When God sent
his Son into the world, it was not to reject the world,
but so that the world might find salvation through
him." "I have come to save the world, not to pass
sentence on the world." [109] If he had come as a judge,
he would have worn an air of implacable severity; but
as a savior his countenance, his words, and his actions
all betoken his essential goodness. By stating that he
has come not as a judge but as a savior, Jesus wishes
to emphasize that his goodness, which is revealed in

[109] John 3:17; 12:47.

his various acts of sympathy, compassion, and kindness, is not an accidental or occasional quality of his
nature, but a general attitude which he purposely
adopts in keeping with the purpose of his mission.
This essential goodness of the Savior, which serves to
define him, is an innovation with respect to the traditional Jewish conception of the Messias. The Jews
principally thought of the Messias in terms of his
greatness and the effect which his glory would have;
in the book of Enoch, for example, it was prophesied
that the Son of Man would appear and assure the final
triumph of the righteous over the wicked. The Messias
or Son of Man was thought of in terms of the terrifying victory he would bring about, and no one imagined
that he would come into the world as a familiar friend,
as a good savior. Miracles are what the Pharisees demand from Christ, and he completely mystifies them
by laying stress on his essential goodness. The Baptist
himself is disturbed by this aspect of his nature; he
had prophesied that an axe would be put to the roots
of every tree which did not bear good fruit and that
the tree itself would be cast into the fire. But the attitude of Jesus is hardly reminiscent of that of a wood-
cutter swinging his axe. He replies to the question put
him by John by pointing to other signs as proof that
he is indeed the Messias, signs which speak of love:
the blind see, the deaf hear, the lepers are healed, the
lame walk, the dead rise, and the poor have the good
news preached to them. The picture of the new age

drawn by the Messias shows definite traces of goodness.

At the very beginning of his ministry Jesus takes part at the wedding-feast at Cana in his capacity as the Savior and thereby shows how much he is moved by goodwill towards men. Shortly before this event takes place he had been fasting in the desert, but he now agrees to accept an invitation to a wedding. The harsh regime he followed in the desert was a burden to no one, because he was alone there with the Father; on this occasion he wishes to show his complete sympathy for men and share in their pleasures. How remarkable it is that one who is the bearer of such a lofty spiritual message should begin his ministry by taking part in a banquet! We might have expected him to keep aloof from human rejoicing; instead it greatly pleases him, because it belongs to those whom he loves. The one who knew the heavenly banquet does not despise an earthly feast. When the joy of the guests is threatened by a lack of wine, he is the one who saves the situation. He performs his first miracle by changing water into wine. Only a short time prior to this he had rejected the diabolical suggestion of Satan that he change stones into bread, because this had been proposed with a view to satisfying his personal hunger; it would have meant the use of his power as God for a selfish purpose, so he refused. Here at the feast, on the other hand, it is a question of relieving the embarrassment of his poor hosts by performing a miracle for the benefit of others. So he agrees to use his power as the Redeemer and make it possible for the guests to continue their drinking. Furnishing wine to the guests in order to prevent his hosts from being embarrassed may seem to be much less important than healing the blind, the lepers, or the lame, or converting sinners, or restoring life to dead bodies; but it is the very insignificance of this action which makes it so effective as evidence of his complete goodness. True love is, characteristically, always anxious to satisfy the humblest needs or desires of the person loved. The incident at Cana shows the extent to which Jesus is prepared to go in his sympathy for men and appears as a sort of touchstone of his love.

He is not concerned to save merely the rejoicing at the banquet, he also wishes to save the marriage itself. By accepting the invitation of the married couple he puts the stamp of his approval on their marriage. The significance of his approval can be better understood if we remember that Christ has just separated his apostles from their families by summoning them to follow him and that he proclaims the excellence of a life of chastity and virginity adopted for the sake of the kingdom of God. But this ideal, which he himself embodies, does not cause him to despise marriage; there is never the slightest suggestion that he disapproves of those who are not able to live up to this high standard. On the contrary, he rejoices in the happiness of the bride and groom at Cana and contrives to promote their happiness by substituting for the natural wine which is soon exhausted his own

174

wine, which is inexhaustible and much better, thus symbolizing his desire to replace the natural love of marriage, which tends to burn out much too soon, by his own love, a love of an entirely different kind. This symbolical act saves the marriage. His substitution of something good for something that was less good on this occasion is basically the same kind of transformation which takes place in all his friendships; human strength is forced to admit its own weakness and give way to divine strength. Jesus shows his goodness by nourishing marriage with his own love; the unique and transcendent bridegroom imparts to the husband and wife a bridegroom's love, which differs from the frailty of mere human passion by reserving its sweetest wine for the last.

Christ also approaches the Samaritan woman as a savior rather than as a judge. The new law which he promulgates to his disciples is aimed at strengthening the indissolubility of the marriage bond; but this does not prevent him from showing his kindness to a woman whose marital status is altogether irregular. He goes about this in a rather perplexing way. In order to make himself known to the inhabitants of Sichar, he picks a woman of loose morals and takes advantage of her curiosity and talkativeness, typical feminine characteristics, to win her confidence and make her disclose her true moral status. If he had acted as a stern judge, he would have begun by censuring the woman for her immoral life and condemned her for her curiosity and talkativeness. Far from despising her, as some of the respectable people in Sichar are no doubt wont to do, he treats her with marked courtesy and honors her by asking for a drink. Her reaction betrays a certain amount of pride and irritation, but he refuses to give up. He does not withdraw the gift God is offering her, he merely tries to make her understand that that is what it really is: "If thou knewest what it is God gives, and who this is that is saying to thee, Give me drink, it would have been for thee to ask him instead, and he would have given thee living water." [110] This reply reveals the true heart of Jesus. He finds himself in the position of one who ought to be giving, but the rôles are reversed and he is the one who is begging for a drink: "Give me drink."

When he finally convinces the woman that there is something he has to give her by promising her the living water of everlasting life, he begins to make her understand what the nature of this gift is. As soon as the Samaritan woman says: "Give me water such as that," he comes to the real point: "Go home, fetch thy husband, and come back here." [111] Just as he wished to replace the wine at the feast with his own wine, so he now wishes to replace the water from the well with another water. Whereas it was possible for him at Cana to approve of a moral condition which already existed, in the case of this woman he must first restore her moral condition to its rightful status. After having been confronted by love in marriage at Cana, he now comes face to face with love outside

[110] John 4:10.   [111] John 4:15, 16.

176

marriage in the person of this woman. He wishes to persuade the woman to give up her unlawful love, be reconciled with her husband and resume her life with him again. Then and then only will it be possible for her to receive the living water he desires to give her; instead of being a slave to her forbidden love, she will then be free to devote herself to the superior love which the grace of Jesus will make available to her. In other words, Christ wishes to bring about a complete change of heart in her, as he does in the case of all those whom he loves. In her case his kindness is the more remarkable, because it is shown to a person whose actual moral status he is obliged to condemn and who is firmly told to give up her immoral way of life. The whole purpose of his kindness is to try to save her; to heal an ailing heart it is first necessary to reach it.

It will help us to understand the real extent of Christ's kindness if we compare his attitude with that of his disciples. A village in Samaria refuses to receive Jesus because the inhabitants believe he is on pilgrimage to Jerusalem; their hatred for the worship in the temple is aroused by the thought. James and John react like "sons of thunder"; "Lord, wouldst thou have us bid fire come down from heaven, and consume them?" [112] Christ turns and rebukes them for their suggestion, and then passes on to another village. He wishes his earthly passage to be marked by acts of

[112] Luke 9:54.

kindness, not by expressions of revenge, and he tries to instill this idea into his apostles.

The same thing happens when little children are brought to him to be touched and blessed. His disciples object to this and try to prevent them from approaching, on the grounds that the Master has more important things to do than to embrace little children. Jesus becomes indignant and says to his apostles: "Let the children come to me . . . do not keep them back; the kingdom of God belongs to such as these." [113] Whereupon he embraces them and then bestows his blessing upon them. He is first moved by his tender love for them and must draw them to his heart before placing his hands on them. This action is typical of his attitude throughout his career; he first loves, then sanctifies and saves.

On another occasion John's attitude appears to be rather unkind and even marked by a certain amount of jealousy; he says: "Master, we saw a man who does not follow in our company casting out devils in thy name, and we forbade him to do it." Christ will not hear of this: "Forbid him no more; no one who does a miracle in my name will lightly speak evil of me. The man who is not against you is on your side." [114] Jesus not only does not sympathize with the narrow point of view of his disciple, but prefers as a matter of principle to put the most charitable interpretation possible on the other man's action. He is anxious to preserve and to save whatever can be saved in man.

[113] Mark 10:14.   [114] Mark 9:37, 38–39.

At Jericho a blind man cries after him: "Jesus, son of David, have pity on me!" [115] His cries annoy the crowd surrounding Jesus and some try to silence him, but the man only cries all the louder, until Jesus finally has him brought to him. Once again he shows that his goodness is more profound than that of his followers, and that he is always prepared to go farther than they in showing patience and goodwill towards others.

His pity

His rôle as Savior is especially evident in his great pity for others. Jesus could have refused to show any pity when he encountered human misery, because he knew that the only evil which men have to fear is sin and that physical suffering is not something evil in itself, but is meant to purify and elevate the soul; it is intended to strip the heart of too much attachment to earthly things and cause it to place all its confidence and hope in God alone. Jesus himself will follow a road of suffering to the very end and will achieve man's redemption in this way. During his public life he is constantly aware that the road he is following will lead to his passion and that he has been sent into the world for the very purpose of taking on himself the sorrows of the cross. Since he voluntarily agrees to bear this burden, it would seem logical for him not to have to assume the burden of each man's sorrow as he encounters him; would it not be possible for him to

[115] Mark 10:47.

ensure the spiritual welfare of mankind by refusing to take part in man's suffering and by merely encouraging him to bear it nobly and courageously? In his Sermon on the Mount he declares that those who are afflicted or persecuted are blessed. Why should he be obliged to dry the tears of those who weep or relieve the torments of those who suffer?

Actually, he is far from being insensible to these things. The rôle he is destined to play on Calvary and his doctrine of redemption through suffering incline him to be moved by human suffering and make him anxious to relieve it. His heart speaks out whenever it encounters grief of this sort. We have already seen how he could not restrain his tears at Bethany, when he saw the grief of Martha, Mary, and the others. He is less moved by the sight of a funeral procession in the streets of Naim than he is by the sobbing of the widow who has lost her only son. Her sorrow touches Jesus to such an extent that he feels impelled to put an end to it, unable to bear the spectacle of her tears: "Do not weep." He puts his hand on the bier and stops those who are carrying it. "Young man, I say to thee, rise up!" The dead man sits up, begins to speak, and Jesus, according to the Gospel, "gave him back to his mother." [116] The eagerness of Jesus to give the boy back to his mother helps explain why he was so anxious to show himself to Mary after his resurrection. The account in the Gospel clearly shows that this miracle was performed not for the sake of the boy, but

[116] Luke 7:13–15.

180

because Jesus took pity on the mother. If the boy's fate had moved him, he would simply have stopped the bier and commanded him to rise. The sight of the widow is what affected him; she is the one for whom he has reassuring words and the one to whom he restores the boy. There could be no doubt about the motive for his action.

His attitude is the same towards those who suffer from bodily ills. He has pity on lepers, the blind, and all the sick and weak who come to him; he cures them all. He tries, of course, to see to it that they derive some spiritual benefit from their cure, for he asks them to believe and have confidence in him; and sometimes he declares that their sins are forgiven. But he is genuinely moved by their physical suffering. When they bring him an epileptic boy and he looks at his convulsions, he asks the father of the unfortunate boy: "How long has this been happening to him?" [117] He shares the boy's pain before he puts an end to it. When he cures the deaf and dumb man he raises his eyes towards heaven and sighs, as if to carry the entreaty of the sick man to the Father and interest all heaven in his plight.[118] This pity sometimes induces him to heal even those who do not ask to be healed themselves. One Sabbath, when he is preaching in one of the synagogues, he sees a woman who is bent down and can hardly look up at him, so he calls her to him and says: "Woman, . . . thou art rid of thy infirmity." [119]

[117] Mark 9:20.
[118] Cf. Mark 7:34.
[119] Luke 13:12.

He puts his hands on her, and immediately she is raised upright. The miraculous cures which he makes along the way are the ones which make the greatest impression on the people; for these manifestations of his power are not performed for the sake of exalting himself, but in order to benefit others. According to St. Mark the people were "more than ever astonished; he has done well, they said, in all his doings; he has made the deaf hear, and the dumb speak." [120] The goodness of Christ and the real purpose behind all his miracles could not be summed up in a better way than this.

He not only combats sickness but avenges the honor of those who are sick. When he encounters a man who has been blind from birth, his disciples assume that the man is suffering because of some moral defect or sin: "Master, was this man guilty of sin, or was it his parents, that he should have been born blind?" Jesus answers: "Neither he nor his parents were guilty . . . it was so that God's action might declare itself in him." [121] He thereupon restores the man's sight. Christ's answer is intended to show that sickness is not to be attributed to sin, but that it has another meaning: it is allowed so that the divine glory may be made more evident. In this particular case the glory consists in the power of Jesus as the Messias, which is made evident in the healing of the man's blindness. But the case also has a symbolical meaning and is intended to enunciate a general principle. Christ

[120] Mark 7:37. [121] John 9:2–3.

is giving a new meaning to suffering; whereas it had formerly been accepted as a sign of sin and punishment, he now makes it a divine gift, intended to reveal the splendor of God's power. This is an important point to remember in connection with Christ's love for the sick and the weak. He completely transforms the meaning of bodily suffering by associating it with the great purpose of his love, which aims at giving more of himself to mankind. Suffering appears henceforth as a special sign of God's love and goodness. Christ could give no greater comfort to those who suffer than to allow them to understand that their suffering is the result of divine favor.

Savior of the crowd

Christ's mercy is not confined to individuals; he also takes pity on the crowd. He takes pity on the multitude which has been following him for several days, because they have nothing to eat; he performs the miracle of the multiplication of the loaves in order to satisfy their humble needs. We must think of all the people who have ever been tormented by the pangs of hunger from the beginning of mankind to our own time if we wish to get some idea of the tremendous depth of Christ's pity for the crowd and the great generosity which caused him to distribute food to them. Christ was fully conscious of the material needs of the people and could not bear the sight of those who were hungry. "I am moved with pity for the multitude; it is three days now since they have been in attendance on me, and they have nothing to eat. If I send them back to their homes fasting, they will grow faint on their journey; some of them have come from far off." [122] According to the account of the first multiplication of the loaves the disciples propose an easy solution of the problem at the expense of the crowd: "His disciples came to him and said, This is a lonely place, and it is already late; give them leave to go to the farms and villages round about, and buy themselves food there." But Christ did not have the heart to send his hearers away; instead he causes his disciples to share his feeling of pity by saying to them: "It is for you to give them food to eat." [123] Whereupon he furnished them with the means of feeding all the crowd.

The pity of Jesus is not confined to the material needs of the crowd; he is moved by greater pity for their spiritual needs. The multiplication of the loaves is meant to foreshadow the distribution of the Eucharistic Bread. Christ is particularly aware of spiritual misery, which is the most profound and agonizing kind of misery in that it is very often not perceived as such; this is the kind of misery he is most anxious to alleviate. To those who suffer spiritually he will offer the most precious gift he has, his own body and blood. He is impressed by the spiritual need of the crowd when he sees the people follow him into the desert. He sets out in a ship with the twelve apostles to get ahead of the crowd, but when he emerges from the

[122] Mark 8:2–3.   [123] Mark 6:35–37.

184

ship he notices that they have arrived before him. They have guessed where it was that he intended to go and have come by land. "Jesus . . . took pity on them, since they were like sheep that have no shepherd." [124] Impressed by their desire to follow him and hear him as the only person in whom they have confidence, Jesus gives up his idea of evading them and begins to teach them at length. This is not the first time he has noticed the eagerness of the crowd to attach itself to him, but it is the first time he interprets this eagerness as a sign of their pathetic spiritual hunger and confusion. In their longing for a better life the crowds are desperately looking for someone to guide them, someone to show them the way and instruct them. So far only hirelings and thieves have exploited the people; the Pharisees have nothing but contempt for them and try to influence them only for their own purposes; they insist on imposing on them all kinds of observances which tend to weigh them down. The crowds long to escape from this burden and are looking for a savior.

In his compassion Jesus offers them himself: "Come to me, all you that labour and are burdened; I will give you rest." [125] The rest which Christ offers them is the same kind of rest which caravans wandering over the desert hope to find at an oasis. The appearance of the oasis, however, can be an illusion and may turn out to be nothing more than a mirage. Job compared his friends to fleeting torrents which run in

[124] Mark 6:34.   [125] Matt. 11:28.

the desert and are soon dried up: "Nay, fickle streams, bethink you of the wayfarers from Thema, the thirsty pilgrims of Saba! Some hope I had in my friends, but all is disappointment; with eyes that will not meet mine, they come to visit me. Ay, you have come, but finding me so sorely smitten you dread my company." [126] What a disappointment for a caravan that has travelled all day under the weight of the desert sun to find that the refreshment it expected to find at an oasis is only a mirage! Job wanders in the desert and can find no place of refreshment; the refuge which he hoped to find with his friends turns out to be illusory. Christ takes pity on the crowds which have been wandering for so long in a desert, where all is mirage, and is finally able to offer them a true oasis in himself. His rest and his alone is capable of relieving them from the weariness of the road; his friendship alone can support them in misfortune. He offers rest especially to the Jewish multitude, which is invited to place all its hope in him instead of being weighed down by the numerous, vexing prescriptions of the Law. Instead of the disillusions of the past, he offers to satisfy man's longing for spiritual peace and rest from labor; they have only to apply to him. His mercy is alone capable of providing relief for souls that suffer.

Help for sinners

Jesus is especially moved to pity by sinners, because his love for them is so great. If we would under-

[126] Job 6:19–21.

stand the shock or scandal which Christ's attitude to
sinners caused Jewish minds, we must remember that
the ideal which the Jews attempted to follow was that
of the just man, who was a perfect observer of the
Law. The just man was a friend of God and found
favor with him, because he fulfilled the Law of the
Most High. The sinner, on the other hand, was God's
enemy, on whom he visited his anger and vengeance,
and who therefore deserved no pity. According to the
Old Testament, Jave inspired his people with a horror
for sin, but this horror was very soon applied to the
sinner himself. In some of the psalms the just are
recommended to God for their hatred of sinners, and
they glory in the fact that they have broken off all
relations with those who are wicked. This avoidance
of all contact with sinners later assumed a ritualistic
significance. Jesus shows his dislike for this ritual ostra-
cism of sinners in a decisive and positive way by publicly associating with them and even by going so far
as to dine in their homes. His enemies contemp-
tuously charge him with being a "friend of publicans
and sinners." [127] When the Pharisees charge him with
this and ask his disciples: "How comes it that your
master eats with publicans and sinners?" Jesus himself
answers them: "I have come to call sinners, not the
just." [128] He also gives the profound reason for his attitude: "It is not those who are in health that have
need of the physician, it is those who are sick. Go
home and find out what the words mean, It is mercy

[127] Matt. 11:19.　　　　[128] Matt. 9:11, 13.

187

that wins favour with me, not sacrifice." [129] Sinners
are the ones for whom he has pity above all others,
because of their miserable spiritual condition; his heart
goes out to them, because they are in such need of a
physician.

It will help us to understand the reasons which
induced him to show a special preference for sinners
if we remember the picture which was constantly
before his eyes and the fact that the real state of souls
was apparent to him. The Pharisees, on the one hand,
are proud of their alleged perfection, having nothing
to learn and nothing to ask forgiveness for: "I thank
thee, God, that I am not like the rest of men, who
steal and cheat and commit adultery, or like the publican here; for myself, I fast twice in the week, I give
tithes of all that I possess." They have no need of a
savior. The publicans, on the other hand, do not dare
to raise their eyes to heaven, but beat themselves on
the breast, saying: "God, be merciful to me; I am a
sinner." [130] It is not difficult to see why Christ should
feel more sympathy for the latter. The two attitudes
are constantly before his eyes and he finds evidence of
them wherever he goes. The feast in the house of
Simon the Pharisee is a good example of this. On this
occasion Christ is aware of being spied upon by a man
who is trying to judge him on the basis of his own
superiority; the man's courtesy has been marked by
none of the signs which would indicate that he has
any respect or feeling of cordiality for Jesus. Suddenly

[129] Matt. 9:12–13.　　　　　[130] Luke 18:11–12, 13.

a woman enters the door. She hardly dares to raise her eyes from the floor. It is obvious that she must have exerted pressure to enter a room where only men are supposed to be admitted, contrary to all custom; she is both indignant and excited and her heart seems about to break. She goes straight to Jesus and seeks asylum with him. The Master then turns towards her with a look full of compassion and love, and she is saved. She has placed all her hopes in him and this has saved her. Like the publican in the parable she finds more favor with him than the Pharisee.[131] That is why Christ says to the Pharisees: "The publicans and the harlots are further on the road to God's kingdom than you." [132]

We have noticed the way in which Christ's friendships bring about a change of heart in those who become his friends. The kindness he shows to the repentant sinner on this occasion also brings about a complete change in her. The moment she reaches the side of Jesus she is able to sense from his kindly attitude that she is welcome and forgiven. His kindness affects her to such an extent that she bursts into tears. The tears flow freely over the Master's feet and when she has recovered herself somewhat, she loosens her hair and wipes the feet she has just washed with her tears of repentance and gratitude. Encouraged by the kindness of the Savior, she dares to do something she would never have thought possible, she kisses his feet. A sinner allowed to touch a holy man and kiss

[131] Cf. Luke 7:36–50.   [132] Matt. 21:31.

his feet! Finally, she pours over his feet the scented ointment, which she has brought with her in an alabaster vase. This whole display of affection naturally follows from certain signs, not expressly mentioned in the Gospel, whereby Jesus must have indicated to her that he approved of what she was doing. As soon as she is aware of this approval, the woman is prepared to devote her whole heart to Jesus; she whose life had hitherto been so full of joy and laughter now begins to weep. The hair which had so often been loosed in immorality serves humbly to wipe the Master's feet. Her kisses which had formerly been so shamelessly abused are now inspired by the purest of motives. The sweet smelling ointments which had formerly been used for purposes of seduction become the mark of her repentance. Everything which had formerly been used for sin is henceforth devoted to Christ; the Master's kindness has succeeded in transforming her degrading passion into a sincere and holy love.

His goodness also produces a similar change of heart in Zacchaeus, whose curiosity prompts him to climb into a sycamore tree to get a better view of Jesus. The effort in itself shows that he is interested to see one about whom such marvelous things have been told. Christ is therefore anxious not to lose the opportunity of rewarding him for his friendly disposition, timid and imperfect though it is. "Zacchaeus, he said, make haste and come down; I am to lodge to-day at thy house." [133] Zacchaeus is one of the chief

[133] Luke 19:5.

publicans, who has enriched himself by financial ex-
actions at the expense of the people and is probably
one of the most hated men in Jericho. Despite this, he
is the one chosen by Christ for this honor. Zacchaeus
himself is fully aware of the boldness of the Master's
gesture of kindness, which no doubt gives rise to mur-
muring in the crowd. He is delighted that Jesus has
not rejected him outright, as so many of his neighbors
have done, but openly shows his sympathy for him
and considers him worthy of being loved and honored.
So he hurries down from the tree and runs to his house
to receive Christ. He has been so completely stunned
by the latter's kindness that it has brought about a
complete change of heart in him; he greets Christ at
the door and solemnly declares that from that moment he intends to give half of his possessions to the
poor and make restitution fourfold to those whom he
has wronged in the past. Christ then turns to him and
says: "To-day, salvation has been brought to this
house; he too is a son of Abraham. That is what the
Son of Man has come for, to search out and to save
what was lost." [134]

Christ is not afraid to display his sympathy for
those who are scorned as sinners. The scribes and
Pharisees are well aware of this tendency and will
attempt to take advantage of it to destroy him. They
bring before him a woman who has been caught committing adultery, because they know that Jesus will
probably be inclined to show mercy to her as is his

[134] Luke 19:10.

wont, and they hope in this way to force him to take a stand in opposition to the Law: "Master, they said, this woman has been caught in the act of adultery. Moses, in his law, prescribed that such persons should be stoned to death; what of thee, what is thy sentence?" The Pharisees are right; Christ is moved by pity for her and wishes to come to her defense, but he does so by reducing her accusers to silence and by putting them to flight: "Whichever of you is free from sin shall cast the first stone at her." When the Pharisees are gone, he says to the woman: "Woman, where are thy accusers? Has no one condemned thee?" "No one, Lord," she says. Whereupon he says: "I will not condemn thee either. Go and do not sin again henceforward." [135] The one who alone has never committed any sin and alone would have the right to condemn her is the first to forgive. The words: "Whichever of you is free from sin," are the key to the greatness of his attitude. Innocent, holy, and absolutely pure himself, he has a feeling of revulsion and horror for sin which no mere man could possibly have, because this feeling equals the force of his love for the Father. All sin is abominable and monstrous in his sight. The woman's crime is capable of arousing only a feeling of abhorrence, but for her person he has only love; the more he hates sin, the more he loves those who have sinned. There could be no doubt about his condemnation of sin; his whole life was dedicated to making this point perfectly clear; but at the same time he is

[135] John 8:1–11.

anxious to save those who have sinned, and his life is dedicated to ensuring their salvation. Hence he tells the woman: "Sin no more," thus indicating that he disapproves of her fault, but at the same time hopes that she will be prevented from sinning in the future; he saves her from stoning in order to save her from sin. The case of this woman has been cited ever since as a classic example of the goodness and the confidence of the Master.

His mercy for sinners is also displayed in characteristic fashion on the cross. One of the thieves condemned to die for his misdeeds along with Jesus defends him from the insults of his companion: ". . . but this man has done nothing amiss." Then he says to Christ: "Lord, remember me when thou comest into thy kingdom." This request does not erase the fact that he has spent a whole lifetime in committing misdeeds for which he is now being justly punished. How many earthly judges would have grave misgivings about any such conversion as this! But Christ has far greater compassion than they do and therefore a much deeper understanding of human hearts; he hears the man's prayer and grants him a reward which all might envy: "I promise thee, this day thou shalt be with me in Paradise." [136] A life spent in robbing and murdering is suddenly transformed by the goodness and generosity of Christ, who is willing to take the thief along with him to paradise on the basis of this single expression of love and faith. Heaven was promised to no one

[136] Luke 23:39–43.

else by Jesus on the very day of his death. What men would have considered utterly impossible Christ achieved by transforming the thief at one stroke into a saint; he wished to show that nothing can limit the power of his goodness.

Christ continues to show his preference for sinners even after his resurrection. The Gospel tells us that his first appearance was made to Mary Magdalen, the sinner who had once been possessed by seven devils. The first disciple he meets is the one who had denied him and wept over his fault. In remembrance of this threefold denial and his threefold expression of faith Christ appoints Peter to be the head of his Church. The one who is blinded by his light on the road to Damascus is the greatest persecutor of his Church.

Why did he show such favor to sinners? Because they are the reason for the appearance of the Son of God on earth and the reason why he undertook that foolish work of his love, man's redemption. He belongs to them; he is devoted to them; he honors them and gives them his love. This is all explained in one of his parables. When the Pharisees complain: "Here is a man . . . that entertains sinners, and eats with them," he tells them: "If any of you owns a hundred sheep, and has lost one of them, does he not leave the other ninety-nine in the wilderness, and go after the one which is lost, until he finds it? And when he does find it, he sets it on his shoulders, rejoicing, and so goes home, and calls his friends and his neighbors together; Rejoice with me, he says to them, I have found my sheep that was lost." [137] By recalling what any shepherd would be prepared to do for his sheep Jesus reveals to his hearers the most precious secret of his heart, the trouble he is prepared to go to in winning back any sinner, even if his efforts ultimately fail, and the joy he feels whenever a sinner is recovered. The enthusiasm with which Jesus greets repentant sinners is the feature about his love which makes the most impression upon men; they are continually amazed to be received with joy by one whose judgment they had all along been fearing.

By the same token, when the good shepherd fails to bring back the sheep which has been lost, his sorrow knows no bounds. Who can say how deeply the heart of Jesus was wounded by the persistent obstinacy of Judas? And what of the sad feelings which afflicted him as he looked at the city of Jerusalem: "Jerusalem, Jerusalem, still murdering the prophets, and stoning the messengers that are sent to thee, how often have I been ready to gather thy children together, as a hen gathers her brood under her wings, and thou didst refuse it!" "Ah, if thou too couldst understand, above all in this day that is granted thee, the ways that can bring thee peace! As it is, they are hidden from thy sight. The days will come upon thee when thy enemies will fence thee round about, and encircle thee, and press thee hard on every side, and bring down in ruin both thee and thy children that are in thee, not leav-

[137] Luke 15:2–6.

ing one stone of thee upon another; and all because thou didst not recognize the time of my visiting thee." [138] Jesus weeps for the stubborn city at the thought of the misfortunes which will befall it. He is not one to rejoice at the thought of the punishment which will be visited upon his enemies, or to demand a disaster of this sort for the purpose of satisfying a desire for revenge; he is moved to tears and tenderness by his vision of the future fate of the city, destined to crucify him. Many Christians will later look upon the destruction of Jerusalem without regret as a sign of God's judgment on the Jewish people for their obstinacy and unbelief. They will interpret it as a sign of the definite triumph of Christianity and as revenge for the drama of Calvary. But Jesus himself could not think of it in these terms; his eyes are filled with tears. He will never take pleasure in the misfortunes of men, even though they be his enemies, and the hand of the Father which is destined to fall on the unbelieving Jews will strike a blow right at his heart.

Christ will find consolation in the thought that this disaster will enable him to show greater generosity to other nations. His rôle as the Savior is destined to assume a much broader significance. When the majority of the Jewish people refuse to follow him, the Gospel will be preached to other nations. Discouraged by the small number of the Jews who follow him, Jesus thinks with pleasure of the great number of others who will be called to enter the kingdom of

[138] Luke 13:34; 19:42–44.

God. His statement: "Many are called, but few are chosen," [139] is not meant to be interpreted pessimistically, but really means that he is prepared to show mercy to many, as the parable of the wedding-feast, at the end of which these words occur, shows. In this parable we are told of the king who is disappointed by the number of invited guests who appear at the wedding-feast of his son and thereupon determines to invite everybody: "You must go out into the street corners, and invite all whom you find there to the wedding," [140] he tells his servants. The newly invited guests, the Gentiles, will fill the banquet hall. In comparison with the small number of Jews who actually accept his invitation, a great many other peoples will be invited to come and sit at his table; there will be many called in comparison with the few who are chosen. Christ will revenge himself for his rebuff at the hands of the Jews by having the Gospel preached to the whole world.

The generosity of Jesus is limitless and whatever he gives to men he gives abundantly, and to all. He never refuses to heal any of those who come to him: "All those who touched him recovered," says St. Mark.[141] When he gives Peter a miraculous catch of fish, he fills the boat to overflowing; when he multiplies the loaves, he sees to it that all are fully satisfied. The servant who is faithful in small things is given greater responsibility and the thief receives the tre-

---

[139] Matt. 22:14.   [141] Mark 6:56.
[140] Matt. 22:9.

mendous reward of eternal life for his change of heart. Christ is not sparing in his generosity; he saves lavishly.

THE HERO

Love which struggles, goodness which demands

We have already noticed in describing the goodness, the gentleness, and the pity of Jesus some of the characteristics which show that his love has great strength. While he may frequently allow himself to be moved by the weakness and distress of those whom he loves, he never allows himself to be moved beyond what may be required or permitted by his rôle as the Redeemer; this rôle is scrupulously observed at all times. But the good shepherd is also a hero, and there is an unconquerable element of strength in his tenderness. In using the word "hero" we intend, of course, to purify it of any unfavorable connotation; Christ never aims at his own glory through the performance of wonderful deeds and never attempts to show off his courage. But he is nevertheless a hero in the sense that he has a profound love for mankind and is prepared to do everything for the sake of this love. Since he does not strive to please men but to save them, his love is essentially a contending kind of love. The heart of Christ longs to win a battle. "Do not imagine that I have come to bring peace to the earth; I have come to bring a sword, not peace." And where is this sword applied? To the deepest affections of men: "I have come to set a man at variance with his father, and the daughter with her mother, and the daughter-in-law with her mother-in-law." Can it be that these alarming words were spoken by one who lives by his love for the Father, is so fond of his mother, is so devoted to men, commends love of neighbor so highly, and approves the mutual love of bride and groom at Cana? Jesus himself provides us with the answer: "He is not worthy of me, that loves father or mother more; he is not worthy of me, that loves son or daughter more; he is not worthy, that does not take up his cross and follow me." [142] Christ requires a love from men which is superior to all other human affections. He requires this above all from his apostles, who have been specially chosen to follow him; but he also requires it from all others, for there are occasions when every one of his disciples must be prepared to sacrifice his fondest affections for the love of Jesus. If Christ makes rigorous claims in this connection, it is not because he distrusts men or wishes to monopolize their affections in tyrannical fashion, but because he desires to raise souls to a much higher level and because he loves them to the extent of wanting to transform them completely by the force of his love.

For this reason his goodness is very exacting in what it requires of men. It is true goodness, which seeks the higher good of those to whom it is revealed, not the satisfaction of mere whims. It refuses to give in to human selfishness, even when this is accompanied by a certain amount of generosity, as in the

[142] Matt. 10:34, 35, 37.

case of the rich young man. The latter, it seems, witnessed the touching scene in which Jesus greeted the little children who were brought to him by embracing and kissing them, and was so moved by sudden admiration for this simple and tender display of affection on the part of the Master, that he rushes up to him with a great desire to share in this affection and seek his spiritual guidance. While he eagerly inquires what he must do to ensure the salvation of his soul, he secretly hopes that a display of meekness on his part will be sufficient to enable him to achieve perfection at little cost. He counts on the goodness of Christ to suggest some easy way for him to follow and therefore says: "Master, who art so good." Jesus immediately corrects this erroneous impression; his goodness is not of the order of human goodness, which allows concessions for human weakness; his goodness is divine, never wavers, never compromises, and is no more indulgent than the goodness of Jave, because it has been received from the Father, to whom alone it should be attributed. "Why dost thou call me good?" Christ asks him. Why, indeed? Is it because the young man hopes the Master will be more lenient and show him kindness more readily than God? "None is good, except God only." In order to show that his goodness is only an extension of that of Jave, he goes through the list of commandments, the essential part of the Law. Then he proposes a counsel of perfection for the young man to follow: "Go home, and sell all that be-

longs to thee; give it to the poor." [143] This injunction
is indeed worthy of God's goodness! If the young man
expected that he would propose something easy for
him to do, he is now thoroughly disillusioned. When
his face falls, Christ makes no attempt to retain him
by modifying his demands; he simply fastens his eyes
on him with a look of love which refuses to admit of
any compromise, and allows him to depart.

In order to ensure the attachment of some of his
disciples to his person, Jesus does not hesitate to refuse
them permission to return to their families before they
begin to follow him. One of them says: "Lord, I will
follow thee, but first let me take leave of my friends."
But Jesus answers: "No one who looks behind him,
when he has once put his hand to the plough, is fitted
for the kingdom of God." [144] The disciple's request
seemed perfectly natural, but it implied a certain longing for previous attachments which would rob Jesus
of his full devotion, so it is rejected. Christ is no less
severe to the one who asks that he be allowed to go
and bury his father. "Do thou follow me, and leave
the dead to bury their dead." [145] Between the kingdom
of God and those who remain outside there is to be
a complete separation, as between life and death, and
these examples are intended to make this point perfectly clear. His words at first may sound rather harsh.
But we must remember that the heart of Christ, which
gives this rule, was full of tender affection for Mary

[143] Mark 10:17, 18, 21.   [145] Matt. 8:22.
[144] Luke 9:61–62.

and Joseph; as a child he had been completely obedient to them; he knows and fully appreciates the value of family devotion with the duties which it entails. He certainly does not disdain the burial of the dead, as he praises Mary Magdalen for her generous action at Bethany in pouring ointment over his feet and interprets this as a preparation for the grave; he predicts that all the world will know about what she has done. But in certain cases family attachment can constitute a threat to the freedom of those who are required to serve the kingdom of God, and so he demands that these attachments be broken off and that even such laudable duties as burying a father must be abandoned. The love which he offers those who follow him is strong enough to enable them to give up these attachments and powerful enough to heal the wound. What he eliminates, he replaces with something else, something much better. His apparent harshness is in reality a much stronger and bolder kind of love.

Christ shows that he is most demanding when it comes to his closest friends. He requires a complete change of heart from Peter, the transformation of earthly hopes into those which pertain to the kingdom of God, and the painful realization, especially for one as forthright and impetuous as Peter, that human strength is weak; finally, he offers Peter the agonies of martyrdom. He requires Lazarus to make the supreme sacrifice and will have Martha and Mary share in his ordeal. Later, Paul will be obliged to change his ways and deny his entire past. Judas counts on remaining with the Master for a time and keeping up his association for the sake of money, but in the end he too must choose; from the moment he makes his choice he becomes a "devil." Christ has pity for him, but will never allow him to "hold with the hare and run with the hounds"; he insists that Judas give up everything for his sake and is prepared to run the risk of his betrayal and final despair. He explains the reason for his action in the solemn warning: "A man cannot be the slave of two masters at once; either he will hate the one and love the other, or he will devote himself to the one and despise the other. You must serve God or money; you cannot serve both." [146]

Christ wishes to appeal to all men, but he has no desire to win vast numbers at the expense of easy concessions. While he invites men to follow him, he struggles at the same time against everything in them which would keep them from God, against all forms of selfishness from pride to avarice, and even against legitimate affections which would mean sharing their hearts with someone else. This struggle is carried on most persistently in the case of those he loves the most, because he wants them to be perfect. His love for mankind is a continual warfare carried on without mercy against Satan, sin, and all the evil passions and complacency of our nature. The work of redemption is a battle conducted on a gigantic scale. The Gospel describes certain phases of this gigantic struggle, and

[146] Matt. 6:24.

we must try to understand the significance of these moves if we would understand the heart of Christ.

The first battle

As the curtain rises on the tremendous drama of his public life, which is destined to be the scene of a terrific and prolonged contest, we see two antagonists before us, and the main purpose of their struggle is being defined. Jesus has retired to the desert to fortify himself, by contemplating the Father and conforming himself to his desires, with the strength needed to vanquish Satan. When the sinister figure approaches and casts his shadow over the thoughts of Christ, the latter is completely absorbed in his love of the Father, which sustains and strengthens him in the desert. He is therefore ready to engage in this first and most decisive battle which will determine the outcome of his whole ministry. The hero of light boldly faces the power of darkness; but no audience is there to witness the duel, because Christ prefers to engage in the struggle with a love which is absolutely free from any trace of human frailty and completely sincere. His heroism is not the kind which seeks to win esteem and renown; it remains hidden in his heart. Men are present in his heart, for he is exposing himself on their behalf.

The first attempt of Satan is aimed at diverting Jesus from his love for the Father by suggesting that he use his power as the Son of God for his own benefit. Since Christ has received his power as the Messias for the salvation of men, Satan is really urging him to use it for an end which would be entirely selfish, to satisfy his own hunger. If in some impossible way Jesus had consented to follow this suggestion, it would have been tantamount to undertaking his work as the Messias for his own benefit, and this would no doubt have resulted in leading a more comfortable life at the expense of those whom he was destined to help. But he will not employ any part of his authority in this way and will not even consent to such a slight exception as changing a mere stone into a piece of bread. He remains faithful to the Father, who nourishes him with his will, and to men, whose salvation is the object of his mission on earth.

Satan tries in another way to induce Jesus to commit a selfish act. He suggests a method whereby the redemption of mankind can be accomplished with relatively little trouble; all Christ has to do is work a few spectacular miracles; let him go up to the top of the temple and hurl himself down before the onlooking crowd, which will be certain to acclaim him for such a stupendous feat. A few displays of this sort would be sure to win him the undying admiration of the people and he would then hold their fate in the palm of his hands. He could attract the whole world to his cause without harming a soul. Christ no doubt compares this vision with the bloody passion and death which are in store for him and must admit that Satan's proposal has its attractive side, for it would free his public life from the constant fear of a cruel and painful death. It would also free men from the disagreeable necessity of having to carry their own crosses and would make it easier for all to follow the message of the Gospel. But it would mean the destruction of his love; Jesus would have to give up his intention of loving men to the very end, to the extent of assuming the crushing burden of their sufferings and wishing to transform them by associating them intimately with his passion. He would be lacking in courage if he refused to give himself to them completely or impose his ideal of sacrifice upon them, for he was sent by the Father as a complete gift of himself and for the sanctification of mankind. The devil's proposal is therefore rejected as a cowardly and horrible suggestion; Christ will not win men by the flattery of miracles, he will save them by the cross.

Finally, Satan attempts to shake the purpose of Christ by showing him the vast extent of his dominion over souls. This power is a reality, for the devil has great influence over those imprisoned by sin. Jesus is fully aware of this great influence, because he knows the depths of the human heart so well. During his years in Nazareth he had ample opportunity to observe how weak and inclined to evil men were; he must have witnessed numerous scenes of human selfishness and deplored the fact that so many were apparently destined to sink deeper and deeper in their evil ways. The obstinate attachment of some to sin could be really frightening, and before he encountered the examples of Judas and the Pharisees he must have been well convinced of this from his experience in Nazareth. Was it not fantastic, therefore, to imagine that sin could be completely rooted out of human souls, when it appeared to be so firmly entrenched? Instead of attempting to restore man's purity and holiness, would it not be better to take a more practical view of the situation and compromise with an enemy who was so obviously powerful and difficult to conquer? Would it not be preferable to win men's hearts by frankly recognizing that they were bound to be influenced by sin to a certain extent? Christ could shut his eyes to this small amount of sin and cover it with the veil of willful ignorance. This is the compromise Satan is suggesting to Jesus, when he promises him dominion over the whole world if he will consent to bow down before his authority. His proposal: "I will give thee all these if thou wilt fall down and worship me," [147] is less crude than we might at first imagine, for he has evoked a vision of the tremendous extent of sin to suggest that compromise might well be in order. Confronted by this deplorable spectacle, Christ drives both the tempter and his suggestion from his presence. God alone is to be master of hearts and Jesus has decided to pursue sin to its last stronghold, to root it completely out of souls, and to destroy once and for all the empire of Satan. He loves men too much to allow them to remain even partially enslaved by their greatest enemy.

All three temptations are obviously intended to

[147] Matt. 4:9.

divert Christ's love from its object, his love for the Father and his love for men. Satan wishes to prevent Jesus from devoting his power as the Son of God to the welfare of mankind; he wishes to keep him from sacrificing himself for them by enduring the ultimate in suffering; he will not allow him to free men completely from the slavery of sin. Satan tries in every way possible to defeat, or at least to undermine, this heroic love of Christ. Perhaps he thought that the goodness of Christ would allow him a victory from mere weakness or complacency. But Satan is the only person to whom Jesus never shows any kindness; Satan is the only one the Master turns away with the words: "Away with thee!" [148] By remaining unshakable in his resistance Christ manages to preserve the full strength of his love and emerges victorious from the struggle.

Conflict with the Pharisees

The contest is destined to be carried on in another form. The Gospels are full of his conflicts with the Pharisees to such an extent that they seem to form the main preoccupation of his public life. Jesus finds these enemies at every turn in the road and their opposition to him constantly increases. As we read the details of the bitter and incessant warfare he carried on with them, we realize the full meaning of the prophecy of Simeon: "This child is destined to bring about the fall of many and the rise of many in Israel; to be a sign which men will refuse to recognize." [149]

[148] Matt. 4:10. [149] Luke 2:34.

This refusal to recognize him will be obstinate and even violent on their part. It is aimed at attacking in his person the kingdom of God, which he has come to establish. "It is the kingdom of heaven that has its preachers, and all who will, press their way into it." [150] Why is their attack directed against the kingdom of God? Why do they persecute him, after having persecuted John the Baptist? The context of the statement of Jesus, as it appears in St. Luke, helps to explain the reason. Some of his hearers do not like the important principle which he has just enunciated: "No servant can be in the employment of two masters. . . . You must serve God or money; you cannot serve both. The Pharisees, who were fond of riches, heard all this, and poured scorn upon him." [151] The Pharisees are, of course, believers in the Messias, but in a Messias who would assure them the possession of earthly goods, such as material comforts, liberation of the Jewish people from the Roman yoke, the establishment of their dominion over other peoples, and a respectable reputation gained through the practice of external acts of devotion. If Christ would only sanction their point of view, promise to safeguard the leading position which they have assumed in the Jewish community, and justify their conduct by being more conciliatory in his teaching, they would immediately rally to his cause. But instead of allowing them to show how clever and accommodating they can be, Jesus forces them to make a choice: they may either

[150] Luke 16:16.   [151] Luke 16:13–14.

209

have their earthly success with all the pride and covetousness that go with it, or Christ as their one Master. Jesus is moved by a sincere desire to save them, but he will never compromise on this central issue; such compromise would be tantamount to sanctioning the corruption in their hearts and doing the very thing which would harm them the most. Instead, he insists heroically on this choice and will accept the risk of being condemned to death rather than give in to their selfishness. This unassailable firmness of his love is what unleashes their fury against him.

Feeling that an uncompromising attitude of this sort is a direct threat to their position, the Pharisees endeavor to find fault with Jesus in order to ruin his reputation. The strange thing, however, is that the only fault they can find with his conduct is the fact that he does good. They criticize him most frequently for the miracles which he performs on the Sabbath. The Pharisees have no sympathy for the joy of the sick and the weak who are healed, but grind their teeth when they see him performing these wonders. They even go so far as to plot the death of Lazarus and would not shrink from such a crime, the very opposite of the great benefit conferred on him by Christ, because of their hatred of him. They have no admiration for the acts of kindness which he showers upon the people, because they despise those who are the beneficiaries of his kindness: "As for these common folk who have no knowledge of the law, a curse is on them." [152] As a matter of fact, these acts of kindness infuriate the Pharisees, because they increase his popularity with the crowds; and this might divert the latter from those who are less generous with them than he is. It is for men that Christ becomes the object of their hatred, and when the Pharisees threaten to stone him he can truthfully say to them: "My Father has enabled me to do many deeds of mercy in your presence; for which of these are you stoning me?" [153] Instead of deeds of mercy of all kinds, they clamor for signs. Instead of good deeds, they prefer to see marvelous wonders, calculated to please their minds, but not to convert their hearts. In place of the love of Christ, which appeals to their own capacity for generosity and love, they wish to substitute a compromise arrangement which would be thoroughly selfish: Jesus is to pursue a more realistic and glorious rôle and give up the idea of disturbing them in their easy ways. Their demand has obviously been inspired by Satan, who tried to persuade Christ to perform a miracle and conclude a bargain in the desert.

How does Christ react to this continual warfare which they wage against him? When they rebuke him for his miracles, he loudly defends the right to be generous; nothing irritates him so much as their attempt to thwart the goodness of his heart. One Sabbath, while he is preaching in the synagogue, he sees a man whose right hand is withered. Will he pay heed to the suspicious looks of the scribes and Pharisees and allow

[152] John 7:49.   [153] John 10:32.

the man to go away uncured, in order to avert further criticism of his conduct? By no means. He puts the question squarely up to his enemies, not boastfully or defiantly, but in order to make it perfectly clear to them that he has the right to heal the unfortunate. He asks them whether it is permitted to do good on the Sabbath, to save a life. When they can give him no answer, he looks at them and then says to the man: "Stretch out thy hand," [154] and his hand is made whole. This miracle infuriates them and they take counsel to find a way of getting rid of him. They cannot bear the greatness of his love.

On another occasion, when he heals the woman who is bent down, the ruler of the synagogue becomes indignant with the congregation: "You have six days on which work is allowed; you should come and be healed on those days, not on the sabbath." He dares not rebuke Christ openly, because of the authority he has just shown in his teaching, so he turns on the people, who are less formidable, and especially on the woman, who is giving thanks to God. The happiness and joy of the woman, which should have aroused his sympathy, only serve to irritate him; instead of joining in her thanks to God, he can only express his indignation for what he considers to be a violation of the Sabbath. Jesus puts him to shame for this hypocritical attitude, and all those who are like him: "What, you hypocrites, is there any one of you will not untie his ox or his ass from the stall and take them down to water,

[154] Luke 6:10.

when it is the sabbath? And here is this daughter of Abraham, whom Satan had kept bound these eighteen years past; was it wrong that she should be delivered on the sabbath day from bonds like these?" [155] While the majority of the people rejoice over the miracle, the enemies of Christ are confounded by his reply.

It is worth noting that the strong language of the Master's reply is due to the fact that his enemies are trying to prevent him from doing good, and are thus indirectly injuring those for whom he has great affection, the weak and the unfortunate. The emphatic way in which he puts his question to the Pharisees about healing on the Sabbath reveals his tenderness for the man with the withered hand, and his indignation at the hypocrisy of the ruler is the result of pity for a woman who has been ailing for eighteen years. Jesus is anxious to protect the other fellow. He teaches Simon the Pharisee a lesson, in order to avenge the honor of a repentant sinner; and he puts to flight the accusers of the woman taken in adultery. When some of the Pharisees accuse the disciples of plucking ears of corn on the Sabbath, Jesus intervenes and says: "The sabbath was made for man, not man for the sabbath. So that the Son of Man has even the sabbath at his disposal." [156] In replying to their carping criticism he not only shows that he has supreme power, which enables him to do good even on the Sabbath, but what the scope of this supreme power is. The Sabbath has been made for man, and since the Messias

[155] Luke 13:14-16.   [156] Mark 2:28.

213

has received all power over mankind, he is master of all that serves mankind, including the Sabbath. His love for mankind is what determines everything he does, and it is for the sake of this love that he comes to grips with the Pharisees. They wish to make the Sabbath a source of trouble, but he will have it be an indication of God's goodness.

His anger

This explains the anger of Jesus, for his gentle and kindly heart actually does experience anger. The evangelists generally refrain from using this word, except for St. Mark, who employs it in keeping with the more forthright language of his Gospel. The basis for their refusal to use this word is easy to understand: anger appears to indicate a loss of self-control, and such a violent passion hardly becomes the remarkably balanced personality of Jesus. But he could and did remain complete master of himself in his anger. How often we find the anger of Jave described in the Old Testament! We must not be surprised that Christ is also angry and that his anger is both profoundly felt and entirely worthy of him. What is it that moves him to anger? "The hardness of their hearts," [157] says St. Mark. It appears also that Christ is reluctantly angry, because his anger is mixed with grief, according to the evangelist. There is some difficulty in translating correctly the Greek term used to express this grief, for the word ordinarily means "compassion"; Jesus is in-

[157] Mark 3:5.

dignant at the Pharisees, but at the same time suffers with them. His anger has this special characteristic that it is accompanied by a profound feeling of pity for the deplorable hardness of their hearts. How does he defend himself against their charges? By healing the man's hand. "And he looked round on them in anger, grieved at the hardness of their hearts, and said to the man, Stretch out thy hand." [158] The anger of Christ thus springs from his love, which is offended by the cold indifference of the Pharisees for others; it is influenced by love, because it is accompanied by a strong feeling of grief and pity; it tends towards love and desires to do good to others.

This anger with the Pharisees gives rise to some of the most violent language which Christ ever used: "Woe upon you, you Pharisees, that you will award God his tithe, though it be of mint or rue or whatever herb you will, and leave on one side justice and the love of God." [159] "Woe upon you, scribes and Pharisees, you hypocrites that shut the door of the kingdom of heaven in men's faces; you will neither enter yourselves, nor let others enter when they would. . . . Woe upon you, scribes and Pharisees, you hypocrites that are like whitened sepulchres, fair in outward show, when they are full of dead men's bones and all manner of corruption within; you too seem exact over your duties, outwardly, to men's eyes, while there is nothing within but hypocrisy and iniquity." [160] For

[158] Mark 3:5.
[159] Luke 11:42.
[160] Matt. 23:13, 27–28.

215

those who cannot understand the language of the beatitudes Jesus has only curses. The violence of his language does not imply a blanket condemnation of all Pharisees; what he is trying to do is to stir the consciences of those whom he has not succeeded thus far in moving or winning over. He tries to shock their hardened consciences by the violence of his language. By exposing the true nature of their thoughts he hopes to force them to abandon their illusions and make it difficult for them to cling to their hypocrisy. What he chiefly blames them for is their lack of love for God and the wrong they do to others. This public accusation is not directed against the individual Pharisee, but against the collective attitude of the group. Christ is careful to show respect for individuals; when he rebukes Simon the Pharisee, he confines himself to criticizing the nonobservance of certain outward practices on his part, and when he replies to the ruler of the synagogue after curing the crippled woman, he rebukes those who oppose his action by using the plural form: "Hypocrites." He condemns the group, but refrains from passing judgment on this or that individual.

This anger with the leaders of the Jewish people is finally expressed in a very spectacular way. The first time Jesus went on pilgrimage to the temple at the age of twelve he was scandalized by the worldly business he saw being conducted there. The worship of Jave was being exploited for purposes of profit, and the Son resolved to put an end to this insult to the Father.

Again it is a question of a choice; men must choose either God or money. When he visits the temple again in the course of his public life, Christ is at last in a position to carry out his long-felt desire; he drives the merchants from the temple and overturns the tables of the money-changers. Those who witnessed this scene no doubt noticed the look of relief which appeared on his face, now that he could give full expression to his love for the Father. This profanation of his Father's house had long weighed heavily on his heart.

This expulsion also marks the beginning of another expulsion, which will occur as a result of his struggle with his enemies. "And this was the admonition he gave them, Is it not written, My house shall be known among all the nations for a house of prayer? Whereas you have made it into a den of thieves." [161] Since the Jewish leaders have permitted the worship of Jave to be transformed and exploited commercially, all nations shall henceforth be called to take part in this service. If the fig-tree of Israel refuses to bear any fruit and is thereby condemned to sterility, there is a vine which has branches for all peoples. The reaction of Jesus on this occasion is a good example of the way in which his generosity is usually expressed; his anger with the Pharisees results in the preaching of the Gospel to all nations. When his heart is confronted by their hostility, it not only does not despair but embraces an even wider circle of adherents.

[161] Mark 11:17.

His goodwill in the struggle

His generosity was expressed in the same way when he said that the Son of Man is master of the Sabbath. The Pharisees had perverted the Sabbath, so Christ gives man a new and more splendid Sabbath. The Jewish leaders had allowed the temple to be profaned and were now preparing to destroy the living temple of the person of Christ: "Destroy this temple, and in three days I will raise it up again." [162] Jesus will offer mankind a much more beautiful temple, not built by the hands of men, in his own risen body and the structure of his Church, which he will support. What has been corrupted and destroyed by his enemies will be restored by Jesus on a more magnificent scale than ever before. The following threat is therefore not merely an indication of his impatience with the Jews: "I tell you, then, that the kingdom of God will be taken away from you, and given to a people which yields the revenues that belong to it." [163] It is also an indication of his intention to make his love available on a more generous scale to all peoples, because of his anger with those who refuse to receive him. He wins the final victory by substituting a much more generous gift for their hard-hearted selfishness.

In this warfare with the Pharisees Jesus stresses that he is not motivated by any desire for personal revenge: "Do not suppose that it will be for me to accuse you before my Father." [164] Moses himself will

[162] John 2:19.
[163] Matt. 21:43.

[164] John 5:45.

218

be the one to accuse them, the one in whom they have put all their hopes. At the same time Christ does not regard himself as the one who has been offended by their failure to believe in him: "There is no one who blasphemes against the Son of Man but may find forgiveness; but for him who blasphemes against the Holy Spirit there is no forgiveness, either in this world or in the world to come." [165] Jesus is therefore not moved by any feeling of personal animosity towards them, but wishes to warn them against the serious sin of refusing to believe the light of the Holy Spirit; anyone who persists in blinding himself in this respect to the very end will not be saved. Christ declares his readiness to welcome all who come to him in good faith, even the Pharisees: "All that the Father has entrusted to me will come to me, and him who comes to me I will never cast out. It is the will of him who sent me, not my own will, that I have come down from heaven to do; and he who sent me would have me keep without loss, and raise up at the last day, all he has entrusted to me." [166] He does all that he can not to lose any of them, by accepting invitations to dinner from hosts who are not congenial and by answering questions which are intended to compromise him. He has words of encouragement for a scribe who shows that he understands his doctrine: "Thou art not far from the kingdom of God." [167] The best indication that he does not intend to condemn the

[165] Matt. 12:32.
[166] John 6:37–39.

[167] Mark 12:34.

219

leading scribes and Pharisees as a whole is the fact that Joseph of Arimathea, a member of the council, adheres to his cause and secretly becomes one of his followers, and that Nicodemus, a Pharisee, comes to find him because he realizes that he is a man of God.

His interview with Nicodemus shows how happy Jesus is to welcome those who come to him in good faith, while at the same time maintaining all the requirements of his teaching. Nicodemus begins by referring to the miracles which Jesus has performed as evidence of the divine origin of his teaching and indicates that he would like to know more, but he refrains from asking any specific question and allows Jesus to guess what he has in mind and carry on the conversation. Although Nicodemus is hesitant and timid to the point of visiting him only at night, so as not to compromise his public position, Christ proceeds to expound the complete change which must occur in those who would enter the kingdom of heaven: "Believe me when I tell thee this; a man cannot see the kingdom of God without being born anew." [168] This amounts to telling the Pharisee that he must begin a new life and change his entire mode of existence. Jesus then explains that men must be born again, because God has been inspired by love to send his Son into the world, so that he might communicate his divine life to us: "God so loved the world, that he gave up his only-begotten Son, so that those who believe in him may not perish, but have

[168] John 3:3.

220

eternal life." [169] The extensive transformation which is required of men results from the love of the Father, who wishes to raise us to a higher life by the gift of his Son. Christ requires the same complete change from Nicodemus which he does from all his other friends. His love for all mankind is just as complete and extensive as the Father's; he will never relax his efforts to win the Pharisees over and will struggle to the very end to make them realize his purpose.

Struggle with his relatives

The Pharisees are not the only ones with whom Jesus is obliged to struggle. His relatives are among the first to oppose him and he must put up with the hostility of the people of his own village, who consider his claim to be the Messias a blasphemy. When he unrolls the book of Isaias in the synagogue at Nazareth in order to prove that one of the passages applies to himself and that he is the one who has been sent by God to deliver the oppressed, his hearers are amazed and refuse to believe. How preposterous, they must have thought, for the "son of Joseph" to claim to be the Messias! They had no doubt heard of the miracles he had performed in Capharnaum, but thought he should have performed them in his own village first. They demanded that he show them some signs. In view of their failure to believe in him, Jesus decides to go elsewhere; it will not be the first time that a prophet has been rejected by his own people and betaken himself to strangers. "All those who were

[169] John 3:16.

in the synagogue were full of indignation at hearing this; they rose up and thrust him out of the city, and took him up to the brow of the hill on which their city was built, to throw him over it. But he passed through the midst of them, and so went on his way." [170] How painful it must have been for anybody with such a sensitive nature as Jesus to see the faces of those whom he knew so well suddenly changed, full of hatred and threats! The Pharisees are not the first who wish to stone him; that urge was first expressed by associates and intimates of his youth!

Among the inhabitants of Nazareth the members of his own family are the ones who are the most skeptical. At the very beginning of his ministry they try to bring him back to Nazareth, as one who has lost his mind, and Christ will have to oppose their attempt to interfere with his work. The one who declares that he has come to separate son from father and daughter from mother is the first to be forced to separate himself from his "brethren," that is, his cousins. But he is firm and rejects their attempt to bring him back by saying that he henceforth belongs to another family, one bound together by the will of God. When they later propose that he go with them to Jerusalem for the Feast of Tabernacles and show himself there for the sake of making an impression, he resolutely refuses to accompany them. He will go to Jerusalem, but without them.

He is even obliged to struggle with his own dis-

[170] Luke 4:28-30.

222

ciples on a number of occasions, as he struggled with
his relatives. The crowds are not the only ones who
share the belief, against which he must constantly
struggle, that the rôle of the Messias is to be an earthly
and glorious one, full of political triumphs; his disciples also cling to these illusions, and Jesus is often
obliged to take them to task for their concern as to
who will be the closest to his throne. He chides them
on different occasions for their lack of charity for little
children, for an exorcist who is not of their company,
and for the inhabitants of a village in Samaria. He
even rebukes Peter to his face, when the latter would
have him abandon the road which leads to the cross.
Sometimes he blames them all for their lack of faith:
"Have you no sense, no wits, even now? Is your heart
still dull? Have you eyes that cannot see, and ears that
cannot hear; do you remember nothing?" [171]

He is really obliged to struggle against almost
everybody, including those who are dearest and closest
to him; we can well understand how greatly this must
have distressed him. If he groans over the unbelief of
the Pharisees and shows his pity for them even in his
anger, how sad he must have felt when even the members of his own family failed to believe in him! The
only person with whom he does not have to struggle
is his mother. But he has to tear himself away from
her when he starts out on his ministry and, above all,
when he dies on the cross.

Christ accepts all the disagreeable matters con-

[171] Mark 8:17–18.

nected with his struggle: the distress which he would have spared others, but cannot, because it is for their own good; and the loneliness to which he is condemned, because he must fight alone against everyone with only one ally, who never appears on the scene. His task would have been much easier, if he could have been more compromising and won people to his cause the easy way. He is destined to appear hardhearted and even fanatical, in the eyes of some, but he knows that men of goodwill will see in the struggle which he carried on evidence of his sincere devotion and affection.

The stakes at issue

It is perhaps easier to grasp the fact that love is what causes him to struggle in this way if we remember that the most terrible weapon he ever uses is the threat of hell. Jesus tries to make an impression upon the Pharisees by the threat of eternal fire; he tries to teach them the importance of love of neighbor by painting a picture of the last judgment, when the Son of Man will separate the blessed of the Father from the damned. This is the true objective of his struggle. The reason he fights so hard and uses all the means at his disposal, including the threat of hell, is because he aims at assuring men of eternal happiness and helping them avoid a disastrous end. The eternal reward in store for them is what makes all his efforts in the stubborn struggle worth-while.

From the first, the contest is conducted on a

gigantic scale and is pursued implacably; the tremendous scale of the battle can be judged from the temptation scene in the desert, which reveals the true stature of the contestants. The intensity of the struggle continues to increase in the course of his public life. The Pharisees are more and more obdurate, and even his disciples have difficulty in understanding and accepting the idea of his passion. As the end draws near, Christ finds that he is more and more alone; he is pursued by his enemies and puts his friends to flight, so that when the moment of his condemnation finally arrives he is abandoned by his disciples and by the crowds, and is spat upon by his enemies. He forces his hearers to choose one Master and, as the struggle progresses, this choice becomes a terrible dilemma: either to crucify him or be crucified with him. There are, of course, many different ways in which it is possible to share his crucifixion, but there can be no middle ground when it comes to making this fateful choice. Those who are not with him are against him. Christ keeps up the struggle until his heroic death on the cross and boldly requires that all men do likewise. He wishes to share with them the love of his lonely, persecuted, and heroic heart.

HIS GENTLE AND HUMBLE HEART

An easy yoke

"Take my yoke upon yourselves, and learn from me; I am gentle and humble of heart; and you shall

225

find rest for your souls. For my yoke is easy, and my burden is light." [172] Jesus is humble in his submission to the Father and he is no less humble in the way he appeals to men. It is a remarkable fact that he gives humility as the reason for adhering to his teaching. He has, of course, many other ways of persuading men to believe in him; he is the one sent by the Father and those who doubt his word are frequently asked to believe in him because of him who sent him; he is the light and the truth, and he urges all those who love truth to hear his voice; he has the words of eternal life, as Peter declares; he guarantees his teaching by working miracles; and everyone of goodwill must admit, as Nicodemus says, that no one could perform these wonders unless God were with him. Yet, when he wishes to attract men and have them follow him, he prefers to give the gentleness and humility of his heart as the basic reason for doing so. His greatest and his most effective appeal comes from his love.

Jesus does not fail to establish his legitimate authority; he does not suppress the yoke or the burden altogether. But he wishes men to be aware of the essential goodwill beneath the burden which he imposes and the authority which he establishes. The doctors of the Law burdened the people with numberless regulations, impossible of fulfillment and from which they exempted themselves; the Pharisees troubled consciences with their formalistic interpretation of the Law; Jesus wishes to avoid all appearance of establish-

[172] Matt. 11:29–30.

226

ing a tyrannical authority over men and makes his law easy to bear out of regard for them. There is no trace in the Master of that selfishness and pride in authority which exalts itself while reducing others to slavery. He places himself on the same level with those whom he is destined to rule, and never tries to make an impression on his subjects by acting in a lordly fashion or keeping them at a distance. He never parades his knowledge. His chief concern is to help men, to free them from the slavery of sin, and to comfort them.

He is truly "gentle and humble." This combination of gentleness and humility is highly significant in his case. Some kinds of humility repel rather than attract. Certain souls examine themselves and arrive at the conviction that they are utterly worthless; they seek to humble themselves rather than to promote the welfare of others; wholly preoccupied with their own egos, they have no desire to express themselves, no spirit of their own. This gloomy and perhaps somewhat overdrawn picture of one kind of humility has nothing to do with the humility typified by the Savior. The humility of Christ is all gentleness and is directed towards others, who are treated in a gracious and kindly way. It consists in placing himself at the disposal of others and thereby neglecting and humbling himself. Jesus is not one to seclude himself in a state of depression, but forgets himself in thinking of others and in being completely at their service. He wishes to emphasize the importance of others, not himself. His humility is intended to reassure others rather than to make them feel ill at ease, and is destined to afford them peace and contentment. We could perhaps call this a cheering, friendly, and comforting kind of humility.

Humility in his hidden life and at the beginning of his public life

The thirty years Jesus spent at Nazareth are an obvious proof of his humility. As a child and as a young man Jesus makes no attempt to win prominence for himself or to display his unusual talents. He knows how to humble himself before others in the most natural way by showing his affection for them and his concern for their welfare rather than for his own. The people in the village take no notice of him and consider him an ordinary person without any remarkable features. They are not aware of the special feature about him which has been noticed by Mary, the fact that he remains in the background of his own accord. He succeeds in conveying to others the impression that he is an ordinary individual in every sense of the word, but the Blessed Virgin first noticed the voluntary nature of his obedience when he went on pilgrimage to the temple at Jerusalem at the age of twelve. This incident showed her that he owed a responsibility to a greater power than that of his earthly parents and that if he continued to be obedient to them it was because he wished it to be so. His neighbors naturally interpreted this submission, which lasted for such a long time, as a sign of his devotion to his parents and as an indication, perhaps, that he was not very self-assertive. All this helped Jesus achieve his ambition: to be little in the eyes of the world.

The incident in the temple sheds further light on the humility of Jesus. He is at home in the house of his Father; he is Master of the Law which the doctors expound. Certain apocryphal Gospels represent Jesus as a child sitting in the midst of the doctors and explaining his teaching to them. But the account in St. Luke presents an entirely different picture with Jesus behaving as a pupil and listening to the words of the doctors. Before undertaking to teach, Jesus began to learn; he was perhaps only anxious on this occasion to show the doctors of the Law what an excellent pupil he could be.

During his public life this humility becomes more pronounced. Jesus begins by having his authority approved by another. He has been sent into the world by the Father, and this divine origin of his ministry would have dispensed him from the necessity of having recourse to any human authority. But just as he wished to be born of a woman and have intimate ties with mankind in this way, so he wished to have the exercise of his powers as the Messias sanctioned by man and to adhere to tradition in this respect. He therefore applies to the Baptist and has himself baptized by him. As far as the Savior is concerned this baptism has no spiritual significance as a purification and does not bring about any change of heart in him. The purpose of John's act in this special and unique case is to mark the beginning of a new phase of Christ's life, his public ministry. The fact that Jesus was willing to begin his work of salvation by receiving solemn consecration from the hands of someone else is a remarkable example of his self-effacement, as extraordinary as the fact that he was willing to learn how to pray to the Father from the lips of Mary. The Blessed Virgin introduced him to the spiritual life; the Baptist is destined to start him on his public life. The Baptist himself is reluctant to perform the rite and wishes to have rôles reversed and to receive baptism from Jesus, but the Savior insists on the fulfilment of his humble request: "Let it be so for the present; it is well that we should thus fulfil all due observance." [173] By fulfilling the "observance" of the old law, John's act marks the founding of the kingdom of the Messias; and the Messias, by bowing his head before the last of the prophets, shows that he is submissive to the old law and has come to fulfill its promises. This human act of consecration is immediately ratified by the Father, when he glorifies the one who has just humbled himself and proclaims that he is his dearly-beloved Son, and the Holy Spirit descends upon him to assist in the fulfilment of his mission. It is obvious that Jesus is really invested with his authority as the Messias by heaven and that heaven will help him to achieve his goal. But in spite of his divine nature he is willing to bow before a man who is the authorized representative of heaven; the most spectacular adven-

[173] Matt. 3:15.

ture which ever took place is destined to begin with a humble act of baptism.

He shows an even more striking example of his humility when he allows himself to be tempted by Satan in the desert. He permits the fallen angel, the very symbol of sin, to approach him and appeal to his mind and his imagination. We might have thought that the Son of God would draw the line at being interviewed by the devil and would have balked at giving him any opportunity to tempt him, as he did; but Jesus is even willing to submit to this humiliating experience for the sake of winning back the hearts of men. He allows the devil to intrude upon the course of his thoughts and agrees to this brush with the power of hell for their sake. In order to destroy the power of Satan over souls, he comes to grips with him and listens to his suggestions. The same humility will later induce him to reveal to his apostles how holiness itself was obliged to undergo temptation for their sakes, for he alone could have described this scene, which no one else witnessed. If he had not given them an account of what had happened, we should never have dreamed that his humility could have compelled him to submit to such degradation.

Humble service

The whole activity of Jesus' public life can be summed up in the words, "humble service." Jesus places himself entirely at the disposal of his disciples and the crowd. Because of his gentle and humble

heart he is able patiently to put up with their slowness
to believe in him and their failure to understand the
true meaning of his teaching; he refuses to drive the
hypocrite Judas away, and he never gives up hope of
winning over the obstinate Pharisees. Even his miraculous cures are performed in a spirit of service and
as quietly as possible. He never adopts the approach
of a magician who is anxious to impress the crowd or
win popularity for himself. The chief steward at Cana
is unaware of the miracle he has just performed. When
they come to tell Jairus that his daughter is dead and
that there is no point in bothering the Master any
further, Jesus encourages him to believe in him, because he has been touched by his sorrow and wishes
to perform the miracle. He takes care, however, not to
overemphasize its importance. "What is this stir, this
weeping? The child is not dead, she is asleep," he said
on his arrival.[174] If he had been anxious to win noto-
riety for himself, he would have acted quite differently;
he might have said: "One can readily see that she is
dead, judging by your weeping; but I intend to raise
her from the dead." Jesus is determined to minimize
the importance of what he is about to do even to the
extent of calling the girl's death sleep and inviting the
scorn of the by-standers.

In the same way the multiplication of the loaves
could have taken place in a much more spectacular
way; Jesus could have suddenly caused a great quantity
of bread to appear before the eyes of the throng. He

[174] Mark 5:39.

prefers to proceed in a much more modest way by replacing the loaves as the distribution takes place. The apostles are the ones who do the distributing. Instead of proclaiming: "I shall furnish them something to eat myself," Christ simply tells the twelve: "It is for you to give them food to eat." [175] He wishes others to share in the performance of a miracle which could just as well have been performed without the help of his disciples and those who had the five loaves and two fishes. He is not anxious to perform his miracles alone. Very often the assistance he requires consists of an act of faith and the healing is ascribed to the faith of the one who called upon him: "Thy faith has brought thee recovery," [176] he tells the blind man whose sight has just been restored. Other miracles end in the same way. Jesus tends to subordinate the importance of what he has done to the greatness and efficacy of the faith of those who request him to perform the miracle.

When the father of the epileptic boy had briefly described the nature of his son's illness and said to him: "Come, have pity on us, and help us if thou canst," Jesus replies: "If thou canst believe, to him who believes, everything is possible." This is not the reply we should have expected him to make. The man has some doubts about his power as the Messias, but Jesus replies not with reference to his power, but to the power of all those who have faith. He thus attributes credit for the cure to the faith of the man.

[175] Mark 6:37.   [176] Mark 10:52.

233

"Whereupon the father of the boy cried aloud, in tears, Lord, I do believe, succour my unbelief." [177] Christ succeeded in concealing his own power to perform miracles so well that present-day readers of the Gospel are apt to pay much less attention to the fact that the boy was healed than they do to the inner struggle of the father and his cry for help in believing. Christ attaches so much importance to this faith that he will not perform a miracle if he encounters an absolute refusal to believe: "Nor could he do any wonderful works there," [178] St. Mark says.

Sometimes he takes special care to heal in places where nobody can see what he is doing. When a blind man is brought to him at Bethsaida, he refuses to perform the miracle in the street, but takes him by the hand and leads him outside the village. Then he restores his sight and says: "If thou shouldst enter the village, do not tell anyone of it." [179]

Christ very often tells those whom he heals not to disclose the matter to anyone, no doubt partly from a desire to avoid arousing his enemies against him, for the good deeds he performs increase their hostility. But he is also motivated by humility, in that he is willing to restrict the field of his activity because of their ill will. In general it can be said that his command to be silent about matters which might have justly and profitably been published abroad indicates clearly that he performs these miracles for the good of

[177] Mark 9:21–23.
[178] Mark 6:5.
[179] Mark 8:26.

others, not for his own glory. They show that the one who endeavored to bring about happiness on all sides through pure love has the profound desire to remain unknown as a benefactor and will not attempt to increase his own reputation in this way. Jesus very often wished to remain out of view, but "could not go unrecognized." [180] In any case he did succeed in keeping the majority of his good deeds from the knowledge of future generations. For all the miracles described in the Gospels, think how many there must have been which have been forgotten! How many lives were freed from sin and transformed as he passed by without leaving the slightest trace, so far as we are concerned!

Acceptance of dependence and resistance

The humility of Christ is also apparent in his attitude to established traditions and civil and religious authority. Jesus has come into the world for the purpose of bringing about a revolution which is absolutely unique in history, and he is fully conscious of this rôle from the beginning. His message is destined to upset accepted ideas and bring about a complete change in men's conduct; he is prepared to found an organization, whose mission it will be to change the face of the earth. But this revolutionary, armed with unheard of power of his own, is content to submit to the powers that be in his own country. While many Jews no doubt are nourishing thoughts of revolt

[180] Mark 7:24.

against the hated rule of the Romans, Jesus does not utter one word or do one thing which could be interpreted as disapproval of the occupation which weighed so heavily on the national pride. He simply accepts political conditions in Palestine as he finds them and makes no attempt to contest the legality of Pilate's authority, when he is brought before him at his trial. He offers no counsel against paying tribute to Caesar and is not afraid to praise the Roman centurion by saying that his faith is superior to any that he finds in Israel.

He shows a similar respect for religious authority. Far from preaching a campaign of disobedience against the representatives of those in authority, whose faults and failings are so well known to him, he asks his disciples not to imitate them, but to follow their instructions. "The scribes and the Pharisees, he said, have established themselves in the place from which Moses used to teach; do what they tell you, then, continue to observe what they tell you, but do not imitate their actions, for they tell you one thing and do another." [181] Christ is particularly careful to place his teaching within the framework of the Jewish tradition; he presents his doctrine not as an abrogation of the Law, but as its fulfilment. He pays the tithe due to the temple, but assures Peter that he has the right not to pay it. He does not resist the soldiers who come to arrest him, and he forbids his disciples to resort to violence to save him. He is full of deference towards

[181] Matt. 23:2-3.

the religious leaders who sit in judgment over him and he consents to appear in the humble rôle of the accused, supreme Judge though he is. He makes no attempt to lead the discussion on this occasion, but lets the judges take the lead, not because of his indifference, but in order to show respect for authority.

In the work of his ministry Christ also shows a surprising amount of humility by allowing the success of his efforts to depend very largely upon what his apostles will do. He makes no attempt to gather the fruits of the great work himself; he sows and leaves the joy and pride of gathering in the harvest to his disciples. On his way through Sichar, while spreading the good news among the Samaritans, he informs his disciples that the fields are ripening and that the harvest is therefore near at hand, but it will be for them to gather it in. If we consider the pleasure he felt whenever he was able to gather in the fruits of his labor, we can readily appreciate how heroic this self-denial must have been on his part. Jesus preaches, but he does not attempt to organize those who follow him on any permanent basis; his Church will only be founded at Pentecost. After the death of the Master, the apostles will benefit from the effect of his preaching and baptize the first converts. Jesus reserves nothing for himself except the fame which is associated with failure. His whole public life is destined to end in the disgrace of being condemned to death, exhibited to the crowd, and abandoned by all his disciples. The apostles alone will be successful and their success will be the more remarkable, because it will contrast so notably with his miserable failure. This is indeed the humility of love.

It could perhaps be said that Christ enjoyed a certain amount of success. The crowd was passionately devoted to him and showed its enthusiasm by wishing to proclaim him king and lead him in triumph to Jerusalem. But Christ did nothing to arouse this enthusiasm; he escaped whenever they wished to make him king. When he arrived at Jerusalem for the last time he did not enter as a military leader, but humbly, as a prince of peace riding upon an ass. The temporary successes which he enjoyed served to emphasize his failures. The wave of popularity which greeted him after the multiplication of the loaves made the general abandonment which occurred after his sermon on the Eucharist the more eloquent. Peter's confession of faith on the road to Caesarea, which was so reassuring, made his failure to understand the meaning of the passion and his opposition to it even more painful for Jesus. The triumphal entry into Jerusalem made the general abandonment at the time of his arrest and during his trial more bitter, and the shouts of the crowd more insulting: "Crucify him!" The transient favor of the crowd was the reason for his undoing. Jesus knew perfectly well that his whole life was destined to end in final humiliation and he strove to bring about this plan of the Father with all his heart and soul.

Jesus reveals his humility in the touching way in

which he approaches his passion. Men frequently consider it a point of honor not to show any fear when confronted by danger, and the heroes of old held that their fearlessness in battle was their greatest asset; but Christ is subject to tremendous fear and gripped by a feeling of aversion, as the drama of the cross draws nearer. The shock of his suffering is so great he can only face it when miserably prostrate on the ground, overcome by the terrible weight of his dejection and trembling with fear. The Father is not asked to test his endurance, but is implored to remove the cup about to be handed to him, if such is possible. Several times during this soul-searching crisis he goes to his disciples and humbly begs for their sympathy. It is his human weakness which he chooses to reveal at this decisive moment in his life.

The same attitude of humility is maintained throughout the course of his passion. How often he told his disciples that those who would follow him must take up their crosses, and yet, when given his own cross to carry, he can do so only with the greatest difficulty. He breaks down along the way and the cross has to be given to Simon of Cyrene. Jesus attempts to set no records for endurance on this road to Golgotha, and the thieves probably put up a much braver front than he does as the procession moves along. When he has finally been nailed to the cross, he refrains from making a solemn speech or delivering a sermon. His few words are breathless and simple. Shortly before expiring he says something which sounds quite ordinary, but which really has a profound meaning: "I am thirsty." [182] Instead of assuming a stoic attitude towards his suffering and concealing his pain, he wishes to draw attention to the torture and emphasize his suffering. Since many of those who are dying ask for water, Jesus does the same; although his death is taking place under unusual circumstances, he wishes to behave outwardly in a completely ordinary sort of way. He is anxious not to attract unwarranted attention to himself even on the cross. Whereas any ascetic would have blushed to say: "I am thirsty," as a sign that he had given in to nature, Jesus has the humility to ask a drink of those who are crucifying him, just as he asked the Samaritan woman for one on a former occasion. Again he places himself in their power, and he shows all those who are destined to follow him on the cross that it is less a question of overcoming the physical torture through fortitude than of bearing it with as much love and gentleness as possible.

Humility in his triumph

The triumph which follows the death of Jesus reveals the full splendor of his humility, so to speak. He could have appeared before his enemies in all his glory, confounding them and causing those who had condemned him to death to fall on their knees in utter terror. His triumph, however, is characterized by a remarkable degree of restraint on his part. Whereas crowds were on hand to witness his agony and death

[182] John 19:28.

NOVENA PRAYER
To Our Lady of the Cape

O Holy Virgin Mary, our most merciful Mother, we Thy children humbly prostrate before Thee, implore Thy grace and help.

With confidence we come to Thee, O Queen of the Holy Rosary; to Thee do we turn our eyes. Bestow on us, we beg Thee, this special favor which we ask.

Grant us health of body and purity of soul; increase our faith and love so that we may know Thy divine Son better and serve Him ever faithfully.

O tender and merciful Mother, intercede for those who are dear to us. Heal the sick, comfort the dying, and have pity on the faithful departed. Protect our families; guard our country; and keep holy Mother Church safe from all evil.

Our Lady of the Cape, may we love Thee more and more, so that one day, united with Thee in heaven, we may praise Thy Son eternally.

Amen.

Cum permissu superiorum.

NATIONAL SHRINE OF OUR LADY
Cap de la Madeleine, Que.
CANADA

OUR LADY OF THE CAPE
Queen of The Most Holy Rosary
CAP DE LA MADELEINE, Que.

on the cross, no one is present to witness his resurrection, and all the guards can remember is that they saw a light and were afraid. When Jesus appears to his disciples, he is not wearing a crown of heavenly glory; he resembles an ordinary person to such an extent that they have difficulty in recognizing him. Mary Magdalen takes him for a gardener and the disciples at Emmaus believe him to be a stranger. When he joins his apostles, he shares an ordinary meal with them. When Thomas professes to be unconvinced and demands to put his hand in the wounds of the Savior before he will believe in his resurrection, the answer of Jesus is characteristically humble; he simply offers to let him see for himself: "Let me have thy finger; see, here are my hands, Let me have thy hand; put it into my side. Cease thy doubting, and believe." [183] The pride of the apostle crumbles before such humility and Thomas is ashamed to insist on being shown in the face of such sincerity. He answers with a profound act of faith: "Thou art my Lord and my God!" [184] The amazing willingness of Jesus to let him see for himself convinces him that he is indeed God.

The last act of his earthly life, his ascension into heaven, is likewise characterized by humility. The apostles hope that Christ is at last about to establish the kingdom of Israel and look forward to embarking upon a glorious campaign of liberation and conquest. But Jesus disappoints their hopes completely; instead of embarking upon a campaign, he disappears from

[183] John 20:27.   [184] John 20:28.

view. He finally leaves his disciples and is lifted up into heaven, but the manner of his ascension must have seemed unspectacular, compared with the glowing accounts of the way the Messias was supposed to triumph. A cloud catches him from their sight. Their last recollection of Christ is typical of the way he has always appeared to them, as an ordinary man making the act of his ascension into heaven and glorious return to the Father appear as a perfectly simple and normal thing for him to do and transforming his assumption of supreme power over mankind and the world into an act of self-effacement.

Admiration for men

Certain actions of Christ clearly show that his humility is essentially altruistic and that he desires to forget himself in thinking of others. This is particularly apparent when he expresses admiration for anything. Jesus is not one of those who seek to humble themselves by disparaging others. He has admiration for the great and beautiful qualities in men and pays public tribute to John the Baptist in one of his sermons. "What was it, he asked, that you expected to see when you went out into the wilderness? Was it a reed trembling in the wind? No, not that; what was it you went out to see? Was it a man clad in silk? You must look in kings' palaces for men that go clad in silk. What was it, then, that you went out to see? A prophet? Yes, and something more, I tell you, than a prophet. This is the man of whom it was written,

242

Behold, I am sending before thy face that angel of mine, who is to prepare thy way for thy coming." [185] Jesus goes on to say that there is no one greater than John among all those who have come before the Messias. This praise is all the more remarkable, since Christ himself does not choose to follow the Baptist's way of life and form of spirituality; in fact, there was a certain amount of rivalry between his own and the Baptist's followers. Jesus prefers to spend his life among men rather than in the desert, and he does not practice the fasts and acts of mortification of the Baptist. Nevertheless, he not only does not disapprove of John's mode of life, he even has words of praise for it and declares his greatness.

Jesus is occasionally obliged to rebuke his disciples, but he also expresses admiration for Peter's confession of faith. He is filled with delight by the little children who come to him and believe in him. He congratulates the Chanaanite woman for her persistence in believing: "Woman, for this great faith of thine, let thy will be granted." [186] He marvels at the centurion who has shown such absolute faith in the Master's word. He is amazed and says to those who are following him: "Believe me, I have not found faith like this, even in Israel." [187] Jesus watches the multitude making offerings to the treasury of the temple and admires the poor widow who puts in two pieces of relatively little value. He calls his disciples to

[185] Matt. 11:7–10.
[186] Matt. 15:28.
[187] Matt. 8:10.

him, so that they may share in his admiration: "Believe me, this poor widow has put in more than all those others who have put offerings into the treasury. The others all gave out of what they had to spare; she, with so little to give, put in all that she had, her whole livelihood." [188] Christ realizes the great significance of what she has done, although men fail to appreciate it. It would be impossible to enumerate all the occasions on which he expresses his admiration. The reward granted to the good thief indicates praise for his contrition and faith in him. The position which he confers on Peter as the head of his Church shows regard for the love which his apostle had for him. Christ goes so far as to express his admiration for all those who will believe in generations to come: "Blessed are all those who have not seen, and yet have learned to believe." [189] The one who delights above all in admiring those who are not very highly regarded in this world, the lowly, the poor, strangers and those who have been condemned for crimes, congratulates in advance all those unknown Christians of the future who will put their trust in him.

In trying to understand the real significance of this admiration of Jesus we must remember that his basis of comparison is the infinite perfection of the Father, in whose sight man's excellence is as nothing. Yet, insignificant as it is, Jesus is humble and loving enough to admire it and recognize its greatness. His

[188] Mark 12:43–44.   [189] John 20:29.

admiration is what gives the actions of men such inestimable value.

Attentions of a humble heart

The humility of Christ is also revealed in the way in which he is concerned with small details which affect the lives of those who are around him. He does not overlook the smallest details and takes a personal interest in them. When he raises the daughter of Jairus from the dead and those who witness the miracle are beside themselves with amazement, Jesus reminds the mother and father that their daughter is hungry and he "ordered that she should be given something to eat." [190] While all are gazing at him in amazement, Jesus appears to be concerned only with the child; after restoring her to life, he looks after her bodily needs. The same love which desires to benefit others restores her to life and satisfies her hunger.

He shows the same kind of concern for his disciples. When they return from their mission tired and worn out and begin to give him a glowing account of all that they have done, his first reaction is to make them rest awhile: "Come away into a quiet place by yourselves, and rest a little." [191] Shortly before his death he reminds them that he has never left them in want of anything: "Did you go in want of anything, when I sent you out without purse, or wallet, or shoes?" "Nothing," [192] they reply. He shows that he is

[190] Mark 5:43.
[191] Mark 6:31.

[192] Luke 22:35.

245

constantly concerned with their smallest material wants.

After his resurrection he shows even greater care about such details. When he appears to his disciples on the shores of the sea of Tiberias, he begins to prepare a meal for them, before they even recognize him and join him. He shows respect for their labor by telling them to bring some of the fish he has just helped them catch and put them on the fire. His heart is gentle and humble to the very end.

The devices of a humble heart

He employs the simple devices of love and finds remarkable ways of bringing happiness to those around him. He falls asleep, as the ship in which he and his disciples have taken passage begins to be tossed by the waves and is in danger of sinking. His disciples are unable to share his calm attitude and awaken him: "Lord, save us, we are sinking." [193] Jesus rebukes them for their faintheartedness; then, turning to check the wind and the sea, he restores their confidence. Their gratitude for what he has done is all the greater, because their fears had been so real. On another occasion, when he walks on the sea towards his disciples, he pretends to go on, as he does with the disciples on the road to Emmaus. The apostles are shaken by his appearance and cry out. "Take courage, he said, it is myself; do not be afraid." [194] We may perhaps say that Christ deliberately makes a terrifying appearance

[193] Matt. 8:25. [194] Matt. 14:27.

on occasion, so that the terror which he inspires may immediately give way to confidence.

The woman with the issue of blood who succeeded in touching the hem of his garment was immediately cured and thought that she could escape through the crowd unnoticed. But Christ asks a question that puts her in an embarrassing position: "Who touched my garments?" The woman realizes that she has been found out and comes up to the Master. All eyes are focused on her and she trembles with the thought that she has secretly stolen a miracle and must now be prepared to pay the penalty for her rashness. She falls at the feet of the Master and confesses what she has done. Jesus reassures her: "My daughter, thy faith has brought thee recovery; go in peace, and be rid of thy affliction." [195] After telling her that her faith, rather than the fact that she has touched his garment, has resulted in her being cured, he gives her the peace of his friendship and assures her that she has been healed with his full approval. What pleasure it must have caused him to see the woman's fears suddenly converted into joy!

This is the normal pattern of his appearances after his resurrection. The apostles are afraid that he may suddenly appear before them at any time, but he reassures them by saying: "It is myself; do not be afraid." [196] He delights in surprising them and converting their apprehension into joy; this is part of the psychology of love. The tears of Mary Magdalen sud-

[195] Mark 5:30, 34.   [196] Luke 24:36.

denly give way to joy when he calls her by name, and he warms the hearts of the two disciples on the road to Emmaus, before finally disclosing his identity.

Before granting a favor, he sometimes gives the impression that he will refuse it. He appears at Cana to have first opposed the request of his mother for the purpose of causing greater joy when the miracle was actually performed. The Syrophoenician woman who comes to beg him to heal her daughter receives a rather brusk reply: "Let the children have their fill first; it is not right to take the children's bread and throw it to the dogs." His tone indicates that he is not willing to refuse her outright, so she persists in her entreaty: "Ah, yes, Lord; the dogs eat of the crumbs the children leave, underneath the table." [197] By pretending at first to refuse, Jesus evokes the desired expression of faith and performs the miracle he is anxious to perform all along.

He employs similar tactics in the case of Lazarus. In spite of the touching appeal of Martha and Mary: "Lord, he whom thou lovest lies here sick," [198] he refuses to come to their immediate assistance. He remains two whole days before going to Bethany. He could, of course, have come and healed his friend even before word was sent, but he waited so long in order to show Lazarus an even greater favor by raising him from the dead after he had been four days in the grave. Martha and Mary also feel greater joy in having their brother restored to them after they had given

[197] Mark 7:27–28.   [198] John 11:3.

him up for good. Jesus knows the importance of holding something back in order to make his goodness seem more generous.

The same principle is applied in the case of his passion. By allowing himself to be torn from his faithful disciples and thereby causing them keen disappointment, Christ makes it possible for them to be more overjoyed, when they behold him again after his resurrection. The empty feeling which they have when he ascends into heaven is soon filled by the fullness of the Holy Spirit; his final departure gives way to the joy of Pentecost.

This game of surprises which Jesus plays with his followers shows that he attaches great value to the joy of others and that his gentle and humble heart constantly strives to promote this joy in every possible way.

HIS SACRIFICED HEART

The supreme gift

"The good shepherd lays down his life for his sheep." [199] Sacrifice is the supreme test of love. Christ's heart is truly revealed in his passion and death on the cross; all the other manifestations of his soul are explained in terms of this final moment and everything he does in the course of his life is made clear in the cruel, positive, and decisive light of this supreme gift. Moreover, this gift is something entirely willed, free,

[199] John 10:11.

249

and spontaneous. The condemnation of Jesus is not merely an accidental thing brought about through the machinations of his enemies; Christ voluntarily offers himself of his own free will: "This my Father loves in me, that I am laying down my life, to take it up again afterwards. Nobody can rob me of it; I lay it down of my own accord. I am free to lay it down, free to take it up again; that is the charge which my Father has given me." [200] Shortly before pronouncing his condemnation Pilate shows that he is irritated by Christ's silence and reminds him of his power: "Hast thou no word for me? Dost thou not know that I have power to crucify thee, and power to release thee?" But Jesus only answers: "Thou wouldst not have any power over me at all, if it had not been given thee from above." [201] The will of the Father, to which he freely submits, is what governs all things, and Christ is fully aware of the fact that he is going to his own death of his own free will. This fact needs emphasis, because there is much more love in a freely willed offering than in resignation to an inevitable end. Christ longs for this fateful end more than he longed for anything else in his earthly life; it is because of "this hour of trial" that he came into the world.[202] Finally, he desires it for the purpose of showing his great love for mankind: "This is the greatest love a man can show, that he should lay down his life for his friends." [203] The whole life of Jesus is directed towards this end, his thoughts and

[200] John 10:17–18.
[201] John 19:10, 11.
[202] John 12:27.
[203] John 15:13.

his desires are turned towards this indication of his complete dedication to mankind. His heart yearns for this moment, when he will be privileged to show the full measure of his affection.

The Last Supper

This is why the hours immediately preceding the ordeal are given over to the expression of his great love; the statements which he makes during the Last Supper are the clearest expression of his love which the Gospels contain. Jesus begins by telling his apostles of his great longing to share this final meal with them: "I have longed and longed to share this paschal meal with you before my passion." [204] He has long nourished the hope, and his desire tended to increase with the passage of time. When he thought of his suffering and the death he must undergo, he was pleased to think that he would have the opportunity of eating a final meal with this group of his friends before the terrible hour of his passion arrived. He had also looked forward for a long time to the institution of the Holy Eucharist, which had been foreshadowed in the multiplication of the loaves and in the following sermon. Now, at last, his desire can be fulfilled. Jesus longs for this meal which is destined to mark the high point of his intimacy with the twelve apostles; and his longing is all the greater, because he is already conscious of the pain which will soon be upon him, and he instinctively wishes to find support and com-

[204] Luke 22:15.

fort in the company of his disciples. He is about to consecrate and immortalize in a very definite way this profound intimacy with his apostles, and he is anxious to do so without delay.

As soon as they are all seated at table, Christ does something which clearly reveals the nature of his love. He wishes to show them that he has not longed for this meal merely for the sake of enjoying their friendly companionship. He has come to the cenacle to give, not to receive, to serve, not to be served; so he begins by washing their feet. St. John expressly states that Jesus is fully conscious of his divine power when he performs this rite: "Jesus knew well that the Father had left everything in his hands; knew it was from God that he came, and to God that he went. And now rising from supper, he laid his garments aside . . ." [205] Before washing the feet of his disciples he is filled with the consciousness of his supreme power; he makes this perfectly clear in the midst of his action by telling Peter: "If I do not wash thee, it means thou hast no companionship with me." [206] Finally, after putting his garments on again and taking his place at the table, he makes explicit reference to his supreme power: "You hail me as the Master, and the Lord; and you are right, it is what I am." [207] He thus washes the feet of his disciples in his capacity as Master and Lord; his supreme power is humbly placed at their service. Jesus wishes in this way to set them an example: "If

[205] John 13:3-4.
[206] John 13:8.
[207] John 13:13.

252

I have washed your feet, I who am the Master and the
Lord, you in your turn ought to wash each other's
feet. I have been setting you an example, which will
teach you in your turn to do what I have done for
you." [208] Jesus is perfectly sincere in what he has just
done and this act reveals the true nature of his soul.
It was not his intention to do something merely for
the sake of setting them an example to follow, any
more than he meant that they should pretend to love
one another when he told them to love each other as
he loved them. When he puts the towel about him
and fills the basin to wash their feet, Christ is moved
by the same thought which inspires his whole earthly
life, the love which causes him to place his divine
power at the service of men. He is fully himself, when
he performs this humble act as incarnate God; the
one who has been sent into the world by love reveals
the secret of his heart in what he does.

This fundamental desire to place his divine greatness and absolute power at the service of mankind is
seen again in the course of his passion. Jesus appears
as both Master and slave: Master by right, and slave
in fact and of his own accord. This behavior throws
light on the essential idea behind the whole plan of
salvation; whereas the divine power seemed to be
rather formidable under the old law, it appears in
Christ to be in the service of mankind. God revealed
his transcendent and supreme power to the Jewish
people for the purpose of making men understand the

[208] John 13:14–15.

immensity of the gift which he intended to give them in his Son. When Jesus leans over the feet of his disciples, he is bending down much lower over them than Jave ever appeared to be higher above all things under the old dispensation. The heart of Christ alone explains the mystery of this divine behavior, of supreme power devoting itself to a simple and humble act of love.

The Eucharist

A similar motive explains his institution of the Eucharist. Jesus exercises his supreme power by converting bread into his own body and wine into his own blood, while the appearances of these substances remain unchanged. He shares this power with his apostles by giving them the power to do likewise. By making use of his supreme power in this way he aims at giving himself completely to men; he gives them his body for nourishment and his blood for drink. He places himself at the service of their spiritual life in the most humble way possible, by giving them himself to eat and drink. He was asked to perform miracles, but this is the most unheard-of miracle of all. The mysterious manner in which the change takes place without altering the appearances of bread and wine serves to conceal the true force of his love. Before offering the bloody sacrifice of Calvary, he offers the sacrifice of the Supper, which enables him to extend indefinitely in time and space the gift he desires to make of himself. He has only one human life and can die only once, but his heart is greater than his earthly life and desires to perpetuate and multiply its sacrifice. He finds an original and mysterious means of prolonging his agony until the end of the world and of continually renewing his transition from death to resurrection for the benefit of mankind. His power is completely devoted to developing his love to the greatest possible extent.

It even allows him to anticipate the hour of his death, as if he were impatient to sacrifice himself as soon as possible. He does not promise to give his body to the apostles; he gives it to them then and there: "This is my body, which is to be given for you." [209] He does not tell them that he will shed his blood, he gives it to them to drink then and there: "This is my blood, of the new testament, which is to be shed for many, to the remission of sins." [210] Without waiting for the following day, Jesus consummates his sacrifice then and there. He does it in a non-bloody way, most revealing of his true thoughts.

Let us analyze his words more closely to discover any trace of his love in them. In addition to the eagerness with which he makes available this sacrifice of his body and blood, Jesus emphasizes the universality of his gift: "Drink, all of you, of this," [211] he tells his disciples, as he hands the chalice to them. This precious blood is offered to all alike and is not reserved for the privileged circle of his apostles; the word "all" includes

[209] Luke 22:19.
[210] Matt. 26:28.
[211] Matt. 26:27.

255

those who will subsequently adhere to the Gospel. He adds that his blood is shed for a great many, that is to say, he foresees an ever increasing number of men in the future who will profit by his sacrifice. His heart is anxious to forget no one at this moment; the desire to embrace mankind in general and each man in particular is what induces him to perpetuate his sacrifice throughout time and space. Christ is determined to give himself in a general and in a particular way; he has each person in mind and wishes to extend to each the generosity of his love.

He declares that the shedding of his blood marks the beginning of a new testament or alliance. Compared with the old alliance, which was sealed with the blood of bulls which Moses sacrificed to Jave, the new alliance is a much greater sign of love. In the one case it was the Jews who made a sacrifice to God through Moses; in this case it is God himself who sacrifices himself and gives his blood to drink by virtue of his own divine power; God is the one who pays the cost of the new alliance, which is concluded at his own expense. As a sign of the new union and new assistance which is being given to men he gives himself, so that when we receive the sign we receive all that it is. The Eucharist is the sign or symbol of the new alliance and the means whereby Christ is given to mankind.

Christ henceforth personifies God's alliance with mankind. This alliance is not a mere contract or treaty specifying certain rights and obligations. Jave formerly promised his protection to the Jewish people in return for their pledge to observe the Law, but he also revealed himself as the bridegroom of Israel and showed this nation the tender love of a devoted spouse. Christ renews the alliance and at the same time renews this tender love. St. Paul will later refer to the marriage of Christ and his Church and recall how: "Christ shewed love to the Church when he gave himself up on its behalf." [212] Christ calls himself a bridegroom, using a term which John the Baptist had already applied to him, and he likens the kingdom of God to a feast which a king prepared for the marriage of his son. At last the moment to found the kingdom has arrived. Before instituting the Eucharist,[213] Jesus declares: "I tell you truthfully, I shall not drink of this fruit of the vine again, until the day when I drink it with you, new wine, in the kingdom of God." [214] He now begins the marriage feast which his Father wished to celebrate for him and shows that he has the feelings of a bridegroom for all those who will join with him in the new alliance; he is full of tenderness and affection and wishes his blood, which is purposely distributed under the appearance of wine, to fill his guests with the deliriousness of his love. A certain amount of cruelty, not very pleasant to behold, marked the shedding of sacrificial blood under the old law. Christ, on the other hand, sheds his blood as the sign of his absolutely

[212] Eph. 5:25.
[213] According to the account given in St. Luke, which appears more probable.
[214] Mark 14:25. His words appear to be more faithfully reproduced in St. Mark than in St. Luke.

pure love. His alliance is essentially an alliance of the heart.

It is also a work of mercy and reconciliation. When Christ declares that his blood is shed for the remission of sins, he has in mind the misery caused by all the sins in the world and the distress of the many sinners who would have no hope of salvation without him. The sacrifice which is marked by the shedding of his blood is the answer of Jesus to this distress and a clear indication of his compassion. At the same time it is a mark of reconciliation, for sin is an offense against God and involves man in a state of hostility to his creator, while the blood shed by Christ atones for this offense, obtains divine forgiveness for man, and does away with this hostility. Jesus rejoices, as he hands the cup to his disciples, that he can bring comfort to so many sinners and reconcile mankind again with the Father. This is truly an important moment in man's history, for his struggle against sin has thus far been in vain, unable as he was to free himself from the fatal tendencies disposing him to evil. He has endeavored to free himself by resorting to all kinds of religious practices designed to purify and to cleanse him of his faults, but he could never rid himself of the sense of guilt. Finally, after turning this way and that in an effort to rid himself of the load of his sins, he felt the full load fall more heavily on his shoulders than ever before. The Jews had offered numerous sacrifices for the purpose of reconciling themselves with God, and the pagans had called upon a great many divinities in the hope of obtaining their aid. All these attempts were destined to end in failure, because the blood of animals had little value and the divinities of the pagans were the products of their own imagination. Christ is at length able to answer man's intense longing for liberation from sin and reconciliation with God, which man had been unable to bring about himself; and he achieves it for all men at a single stroke. Man's desire for reconciliation had been profound, but Christ's love in granting this desire is even more profound. By pronouncing the simple words, "for the remission of sins," he opens up an entirely new prospect for mankind and reveals the motive which induced him to enter the world and to undergo his heroic sacrifice. He is glad to pay a price as terrible as this for the sake of giving such great joy.

In order to emphasize the permanent character of this alliance of mercy and forgiveness he says to his apostles: "Do this for a commemoration of me." [215] This last request from one about to die asking his friends to remember him for the sake of perpetuating their friendship has a very pathetic ring about it. But in this case there is also something more; Christ is ordering his disciples not only to remember him in this way but to perpetuate his sacrifice. He not only asks his apostles to continue to love him but makes it possible for them once and for all to possess the love which he has for them, hold it in their hands, and renew his sacrifice. The remission of sins relates to the

[215] I Cor. 11:24.

259

past; these words look to the future. His love, which was strong enough to assure men forgiveness for their sins from the beginning of mankind and thus satisfy their fondest longing, now turns to the future with a view to transforming them by means of a continual celebration of his sacrifice and to bringing them safely to the end of time. This is precisely the way St. Paul interprets these words when he writes to the Corinthians: "So it is the Lord's death that you are heralding, whenever you eat this bread and drink this cup, until he comes." [216] The Eucharist is directed toward the final coming of Christ and connects the origin of the world and of sin with the final consummation of all things. The love which Christ shows at the Last Supper is capable of measuring this vast distance at a glance and fondly embraces man and history.

Farewell

This magnificent vision, which causes the heart of Christ to swell with a feeling of limitless generosity and allows him to prolong his sacrifice in time, does not cause him to lose sight of the actual situation in which he and his apostles find themselves. The words he addresses to them after the Supper reveal his sincere concern for them. He announces that his death is near at hand. On several previous occasions he had foretold his passion and said that the Son of Man would be persecuted and put to death by the leaders of the Jewish people. Now, however, he speaks of this event

[216] I Cor. 11:26.

much less objectively and in a tone which indicates
that he is about to take leave of his friends. His voice
becomes tender, and his heart goes out to them: "My
children," [217] he says. We are reminded of the comparison he used when speaking of Jerusalem, of a hen
who endeavors to gather her little chicks under her
wing. The same feeling of love characterizes his attitude towards the disciples on this occasion; Christ
gathers them about him in these last moments of his
earthly life, so that they can enjoy the warmth of his
affection. "It is only for a short time that I am with
you." [218] These last few moments are exceedingly precious and he wishes to lose none of them. Christ is no
doubt happy in the thought that he is returning to the
Father, but he is sad at the prospect of having to leave
his friends behind on earth. He has lost his heart to
these disciples with whom he has lived, and it is heart-
rending for him to part from them. He wishes that it
were possible to prolong this earthly friendship with
them, which he has cherished so deeply, but this cannot be. It is at this point that he asks them to continue this friendship with him in another way, through
mystical union with him. This union is destined to be
even more intimate than his companionship with
them during the course of his public life. Jesus once
asked his apostles to follow him and dwell with him,
but now he invites them to dwell in him. They have
observed the way in which his heart has expressed its
love for them; they are henceforth invited to enter

[217] John 13:33. [218] *Ibid.*

into his heart and never leave it again. Jesus tells them
that he will first come and dwell in them, for he claims
the right to take the first step in this union of love. "If
a man has any love for me, he will be true to my word;
and then he will win my Father's love, and we will
both come to him, and make our continual abode with
him." [219] With the Father all heaven will come to
dwell in the souls of those who accept him. Thus there
will be a mutual dwelling of Christ in men and of men
in Christ: "You have only to live on in me, and I will
live on in you." [220] And to show that this intimate
union means the gift of his whole person, he adds:
"Live on, then, in my love." [221] In this way Christ is
assured of a triumph over the instability and frailty of
human things. All those who before his day attempted
to come to the assistance of mankind saw their efforts
come to naught; those who showed their love for mankind were destined to have this love swept away in the
course of time; the great ones of the past have been
forgotten or only survive in the memory of men as a
caricature of what they once were. During these last
few moments of his earthly existence Christ is able to
put the affection which binds him to his disciples on
a sound basis for all time. His love, which seemed
about to pass away, becomes something which remains. His power to love transcends immeasurably the
passage of time and introduces eternity to life on
earth.

[219] John 14:23.　　　　　　　[221] John 15:9.
[220] John 15:3.

The same emotion which characterizes his re-marks when he tells his apostles that he will not be with them for long is felt when he says: "I have no longer much time for converse with you." [222] During his public life he had above all endeavored to train his disciples and inspire them by his teaching, a task dear to his heart, but one he must now abandon. In the humility of his love he conceived of this as an ex-change of information between himself and them, for he does not say: "I shall not be able any longer to say many things to you," but literally: "I shall not be able any longer to say many things with you." His teaching takes the form of a dialogue rather than a monologue. Christ is saddened at the thought that he must aban-don these conversations. But he finds a way to perpet-uate this teaching and shows again that he is able to make permanent something which time was destined to sweep away. "So much converse I have held with you, still at your side. He who is to befriend you, the Holy Spirit, whom the Father will send on my ac-count, will in his turn make everything plain, and recall to your minds everything I have said to you." [223] This Spirit is destined to "dwell continually with you forever." [224] He will enlighten the disciples with regard to the revelation the Son has made, for "He will not speak of his own impulse; he will utter the message that has been given him," [225] that is to say, he will make intelligible to human understanding the doc-

[222] John 14:30.
[223] John 14:25.
[224] John 14:16.
[225] John 16:13.

trine of Jesus and will confine himself to perpetuating this teaching.

This discourse, which is intended to assure them of the survival of his love, also shows that Christ is thinking of the survival of the apostles. When a man is confronted by some great misfortune, he frequently finds that he can think of nothing but the great dangers which threaten him, to the exclusion of all else. But a few hours before his arrest, when his passion has already begun to cast its shadow over him, Jesus is able to think of others. When he tells the apostles of the calamity which is about to occur, it is not merely for the purpose of relieving his own heart that he does so, but in order to strengthen their courage and confidence: "I am telling you this now, before it happens, so that when it happens you may believe it was written of me." [226] He is more concerned with the blow which will fall upon them than with his own situation. In a sermon given several days before, he had said that those who followed him would be persecuted, imprisoned and dragged before judges: "All the world will be hating you because you bear my name." [227] Beyond the present, which is of immediate concern, he is able to look at the distant future and foresee the suffering which his followers will have to undergo. The sermon after the Supper touches upon the same theme. "They will persecute you just as they have persecuted me. . . . They will forbid you the synagogue; nay, the time is coming, when anyone who puts you to death will

[226] John 13:19.   [227] Luke 21:17.

claim that he is performing an act of worship to God." [228] In spite of the threats which hang over his own head, Christ appears to be more concerned with the trials which others are destined to suffer. At the moment when he is about to be attacked himself, he attempts to bolster the morale of his disciples against the future. "I have told you all this, so that your faith may not be taken unawares." [229] He even explains to them the meaning of the trials which they are about to undergo; they are not intended as punishment for the guilty or as evidence of God's anger, but are the signs of the Father's love. In tending his vines he trims off the shoots which do not bear fruit, so that those shoots which do bear fruit may bear it more abundantly. Sufferings are not a sign of divine disapproval, because they are visited upon those who "bear fruit"; their whole purpose is to increase the productivity of the vine. Christ comforts his disciples beforehand by assuring them that their sufferings will be the sign that they have found favor with God.

Finally, before leaving them he literally overwhelms them with his benefits and promises. If he must leave them, it is in order to prepare a place for them in heaven: "Though I do go away, to prepare you a home, I am coming back; and then I will take you to myself, so that you too may be where I am." [230] Jesus thus expects to work for his disciples when he returns to the Father.

[228] John 15:20; 16:2.
[229] John 16:1.

[230] John 14:3.

His departure will also benefit them in another way: "So full are your hearts at my telling you this. And yet I can say truthfully that it is better for you I should go away; he who is to befriend you will not come to you unless I do go, but if only I make my way there, I will send him to you." [231] Jesus makes way for the Holy Spirit. If he had remained among men, he would have made this gift superfluous, for his own glorious and visible presence would have been more than sufficient and there would have been no need for the invisible light of the Holy Spirit to win men over. But this secret working of the Holy Spirit will be a blessing for mankind; Christ disappears in order to make this possible. He is the only man who could ever legitimately claim that he was indispensable, yet he gives way to another for the benefit of mankind.

His departure will also help his disciples to do many things: "Believe me when I tell you this; the man who has learned to believe in me will be able to do what I do; nay, he will be able to do greater things yet. It is to my Father I am going: and whatever request you make of the Father in my name, I will grant it." [232] Christ retires so that his followers may be able to accomplish even more than he has; he will hear their prayers beside the Father and grant them the power to perform wonders.

He anticipates that his apostles will be shocked by what is about to occur. "Do not let your heart be

[231] John 16:6–7.   [232] John 14:12–13.

distressed," [233] he tells them again and again. He offers them his peace, which will preserve them through all kinds of storms. "Peace is my bequest to you, and the peace which I give you is mine to give; I do not give peace as the world gives it." [234] His peace transcends the frailty of human events.

But even more important, Christ gives his disciples joy. Just as there is a false kind of peace which the world enjoys, so there is a false kind of joy which the world possesses. "Believe me, when I tell you this, you will weep and lament while the world rejoices." [235] The kind of joy which he promises to give them is genuine and lasting: "Believe me when I tell you this, you will weep and lament while the world rejoices; you will be distressed, but your distress will be turned into joy. A woman in childbirth feels distress, because her time has come; but when she has borne her child, she does not remember the distress any longer, so glad is she that a man has been born into the world. So it is with you, you are distressed now; but one day I will see you again, and then your hearts will be glad; and your gladness will be one which nobody can take away from you." [236] Jesus experiences in a sort of anticipatory way the joy which he expects to confer on his followers.

Just as he had always predicted his resurrection, whenever he spoke of his death, so he now chooses to speak of the nearness of his triumph, when the catas-

[233] John 14:1, 27.
[234] John 14:27.
[235] John 16:20.
[236] John 16:20-22.

trophe is almost upon him: "After a little while, you will see me no longer; and again after a little while you will have sight of me." [237] He had already given them a foretaste of this triumph in the Transfiguration, so as to encourage them, and now he refers to it as if it were already accomplished: "Take courage, I have overcome the world." [238] The disciples will be able to share in this triumph in the power which will be given them to obtain from the Father whatever they ask for.

Christ leaves his disciples after conferring all these benefits upon them, but he has no intention of leaving them to themselves: "I will not leave you friendless." [239] He is determined to fill up the measure of their love: "All this I have told you, so that my joy may be yours, and the measure of your joy may be filled up." [240] The benefits he gives them so lavishly have all the more value, in that he obtains them by sacrificing himself. His separation from them will enable him to prepare a place for them in heaven; his absence from them will assure them of the presence of the Holy Spirit. In order to give them peace, he is about to submit to the agony of his passion. The joy which he promises them will be paid for by unprecedented sadness; his soul will be saddened to the point of death. He looks forward to winning the victory by submitting to the most disgraceful kind of defeat. When he tells his disciples that they will be able to obtain everything from their heavenly Father, he can

[237] John 16:16.
[238] John 16:33.
[239] John 14:18.
[240] John 15:11.

do so because he has submitted himself to the Father and relinquished all hope of having the cup taken away from him. Christ has only one longing, to bring happiness to others by means of the terrible misfortune about to fall upon himself.

Supreme power and love in humiliation

Christ is overwhelmed in the garden of Gethsemani by the consciousness of his omnipotence. He sees all men before him at this moment and realizes the horror of the sin which imprisons them. This intense realization fills Jesus with tremendous sorrow. His love prompts him to assume the great load of men's faults, and as a result he is crushed by the weight and lies prostrate on the ground. The enormous power of his vision and of his love overwhelms him.

Yet, while his whole being is undergoing this shock, he still shows concern for his disciples. He rises several times and returns to Peter, James, and John to ask them to watch and to pray with him; they have need of help from on high to support them in their weakness. Jesus forgets his own weakness in his concern for the weakness of others; at the most difficult and tense moment in his life, he is capable of thinking of others: "Watch and pray, that you may not enter into temptation; the spirit is willing enough, but the flesh is weak." [241]

The same attitude is revealed when he is being

[241] Mark 14:38.

arrested. On the one hand his omnipotence counsels him to humble himself, and on the other hand he is anxious to show his concern for others. He, as Master and Lord, approaches the group which has come to arrest him. He is the one who speaks first: "Who is it, he asked, you are looking for?" When he says: "I am Jesus of Nazareth," [242] the tone of his voice is so majestic that the soldiers fall back, greatly impressed, and stumble over each other in their confusion. Despite this manifestation of his supreme power, Jesus has no desire to avoid arrest and hands himself over to be bound and led away.

It is with this attitude of a gentle and humble heart that he wishes to reveal his sovereign power to men. He is also concerned about the fate of his disciples. When he offers himself freely to the guard, he wishes to be the only victim. He draws the attention of the soldiers to himself, and when some make a move to seize one or two of his disciples, he says to them: "If I am the man you are looking for, let these others go free." [243] He who is about to be abandoned by his followers wishes to let them escape and seek safety. As he sees them running away, he is sad that they are leaving him, but glad that they are able to escape from his enemies. He wishes the full hatred of the latter to be directed against himself.

His love is not confined to those who are his followers, for this would have amounted to a selfish feeling for his own group. Christ shows concern even for

[242] John 18:4, 5.   [243] John 18:8.

those who have come to arrest him. He immediately touches the bloody ear of Malchus, because he does not wish his arrest to result in injury to anyone. This is the last miracle he performs and it is performed for the sake of an enemy. Henceforth his hands will be tied and he can no longer touch anyone.

Supreme power and love in the final drama

Christ will continue to employ his almighty power in the course of his trial for the purpose of bringing about his sacrifice. He remains silent on two occasions, once before Annas and again before Herod. He is exhibited to the first as a captive of great value, before the second as an object of curiosity. He makes no protest; he is content to remain silent. He could have taken advantage of the interest Herod shows in him, in order to claim his protection and thus escape condemnation; but he prefers to let things take their course.

Before Caiphas and Pilate he admits his supreme power when they expressly ask him about it. When the high priest asks: "Art thou the Christ, the Son of the blessed God? Jesus said to him, I am. And you will see the Son of Man sitting at the right hand of God's power, and coming with the clouds of heaven." [244] When Pilate asks him: "Thou art a king, then?" Jesus answers: "It is thy own lips that have called me a king." [245] But these statements about his power are damaging to his cause; they can bring about

[244] Mark 14:61–62.   [245] John 18:37.

his condemnation. The high priest immediately accuses him of blasphemy and Pilate has the sign "King of the Jews" placed at the top of his cross. It is to hasten the moment of his sacrifice that Jesus avails himself of his supreme power; he delivers himself into the hands of men.

But he still thinks of others. Although he refuses to save his own life, he tries to do what he can for Pilate. His sole concern is to save the procurator's soul. When Pilate asks him the first time whether he is the king of the Jews, Jesus answers: "Dost thou say this of thy own impulse . . . or is it what others have told thee of me?" [246] He suggests that the question has a deeper meaning and that he is king in a sense which might interest Pilate, but that the latter ought to ask him of his own accord, not as judge at a trial. But Pilate refuses to take the hint. Jesus therefore proceeds to explain that his kingdom is not of this world and that it belongs to the realm of truth. Pilate's reaction is negative and skeptical; yet he has obviously been impressed by the innocence of the accused, and the light of Christ has succeeded in penetrating at least partially into his soul.

It is not for himself that Jesus feels sorry on the road to Calvary when the women of Jerusalem weep on his behalf; he is thinking of the sorrow that will befall them when Jerusalem is taken. Exhausted by the weight of the cross, he is still able to think of the suffering of others and is moved to pity: "It is not for

[246] John 18:34.

me that you should weep, daughters of Jerusalem; you should weep for yourselves and your children." [247] He shows the same concern on the cross. Just as his last miracle was performed for an enemy, so his last prayer is offered for his enemies: "Father, forgive them; they do not know what they are doing." [248] His request is perfectly sincere; he is genuinely moved by pity for his enemies. We can appreciate the real heroism of this attitude if we remember that many Christians will be unable to bring themselves to forgive the Jews for what they did and there was apparently even an attempt at an early date to remove these words from the Gospel.[249] Christ not only banishes from his heart all thoughts of ill will or revenge, but actually intercedes for his enemies, and does this at a time when the Father is more likely than ever to hear his prayer.

His cry: "I am thirsty," [250] shows first of all that he has physical thirst. But Christian piety has not been wrong in recognizing that he is also referring to thirst of a higher order. When Christ mentioned his thirst to the Samaritan woman and asked for a drink, he was filled with the thirst for souls. When he expresses the same desire on the cross, it is not merely because his throat is parched and his tongue thick; he thirsts for the souls of those for whom he is dying. This confession of physical suffering is an expression of the most basic desire of his nature, his desire to save souls. The

[247] Luke 23:28.
[248] Luke 23:34.
[249] The phrase is omitted in some manuscripts.
[250] John 19:28.

conversion of the good thief at this moment serves to slake this thirst somewhat. Nothing could be more touching than this admission to men at this moment of his longing for their devotion.

Finally, Jesus shows supreme concern for his mother by entrusting her to the care of the well-beloved disciple, and magnificent generosity by giving her as a mother to all mankind. This last gift comes from the bottom of his heart.

He thus reaches the climax of his sacrifice, having given all the riches of his heart as gifts to mankind. The words of St. John which serve to introduce his account of the passion may also serve to sum it up: "He still loved those who were his own, whom he was leaving in the world, and he would give them the uttermost proof of his love." [251]

[251] John 13:1.

4. HEART OF CHRIST, PERFECT IMAGE OF THE HEART OF THE FATHER

"Whoever has seen me, has seen the Father." [1] Christ reveals the heart of the Father, when he reveals his own heart to us. The least important act of Christ is not only an indication of his love for us, but of the Father's love for us as well. In reading the Gospel we must not allow our thoughts to be fixed solely on the heart of Christ; we must read deeper and try to penetrate the true meaning, in order to discover the heart of the Father.

The good shepherd

When Jesus calls himself the good shepherd, he is at the same time describing an attribute of the Father. In the Old Testament Jave appears as the shepherd of his people: "Like a shepherd he tends them," [2] according to Isaias. The psalmist rejoices that Jave leads Israel "with a shepherd's care." [3] When he complains that all those who have preceded him are

[1] John 14:9.
[2] Is. 40:11.
[3] Ps. 79:2.

thieves and robbers, and when he has pity on the crowds, because they are left to wander by themselves like sheep without a shepherd, Christ is merely repeating the sentiments and mercy of Jave: "As I am a living God, I will have a reckoning for sheep of mine carried off, sheep of mine the wild beasts have preyed on, while they went all untended, with shepherds that would not go in search of them, shepherds that no flock would feed, but only themselves." [4] In the face of this tragic situation, God decides to assume the rôle of shepherd himself: "I mean to go looking for this flock of mine, search it out for myself." [5] He specifies the way he intends to go about this. First he will restore the unity of his flock: "As a shepherd, when he finds his flock scattered all about him, goes looking for his sheep, so will I go looking for these sheep of mine, rescue them from all the nooks into which they have strayed when the dark mist fell upon them." [6] When Christ says that there are sheep outside the fold whom he must bring back so that there will be but one flock, but one shepherd, he appears to be echoing the Father's promise to gather all the scattered sheep together. Jave also intends to provide his sheep with green pastures: "I will lead them out into fair pastures." [7] Jesus grants such pastures to his flock, for he has come so that men might have more abundant life. Jave also wishes to give his sheep rest: "Food and rest,

4 Ez. 34:8. 6 Ez. 34:12.
5 Ez. 34:11. 7 Ez. 34:14.

276

says the Lord God, both these I will give to my flock." [8]
Jesus likewise offers rest to all those who are wearied
and bowed down under their load. Finally, Jave shows
particular concern for the sheep which are lost or sick:
"The lost sheep I will find, the strayed sheep I will
bring home again; bind up the broken limb, nourish
the wasted frame, keep the well-fed and the sturdy
free from harm." [9] Jesus shows the same concern when
he says that he is prepared to leave the ninety trust-
worthy sheep to look for the one that is lost. Jave predicts that he will fulfill his promise by sending the
Messias: "They shall have a single shepherd to tend
all of them." [10] This is precisely what comes to pass;
the thoughts of the Father as good shepherd find a
perfect reflection in those of the Son.

We must be careful not to see in this figure of
the good shepherd a contradiction with the concept of
Jave as a cruel and harsh God. There is no doubt a
certain softer emphasis in the New Testment as compared with the Old Testament, but this difference in
emphasis was foreseen and decided by God himself.
The goodness which is seen in the heart of Christ has
all been received from the goodness of the Father.
That is what Jesus tried to impress upon the rich
young man; God alone is good. The Father is the one
who has given us the good shepherd.

According to Christ, the good shepherd is one
who calls his sheep by name. He thus calls Simon,

[8] Ez. 34:15.
[9] Ez. 34:16.
[10] Ez. 34:23.

277

Philip, Mary Magdalen and many others by their names, and in doing so is merely repeating the practice of Jave, who called those whom he had specially chosen by name. "Abraham," he said to the one whom he had chosen to be the Father of the Jewish people.[11] He calls Moses his "familiar friend." [12] When he calls to Samuel, his voice sounds so familiar the young man thinks he is being called by Heli.[13] Jave even calls all Israel by name: "I have . . . given thee the name thou bearest; thou belongest to me." [14] Jesus' custom of calling his followers by their names no doubt helps us appreciate the goodness of God as manifested in these examples cited from the Old Testament.

It is also characteristic of the good shepherd that he knows his sheep, and Jesus shows a remarkable insight in this regard, inspired by his great sympathy for men. He looks at men in the same way the psalmist said God does: "No thought or desire of ours can escape thy divine scrutiny." [15] Just as Jesus "answers" the Pharisees before they have even opened their mouths, so God is able to converse with human hearts; for he knows the thoughts of men before they are uttered. "Lord, I lie open to thy scrutiny; thou knowest me, knowest when I sit down and when I rise up again, canst read my thoughts from far away . . . [Thou] dost foresee all my journeyings, and yet no

---

[11] Gen. 22:1.
[12] Ex. 33:12.
[13] Cf. I Kings 3:10.
[14] Is. 43:1.
[15] Ps. 7:10.

278

word of mine is spoken." [16] Here again Christ has
more clearly shown what the true meaning of this
divine knowledge is by showing us that it is related to
his love. The psalmist had already expressed confidence in the omniscience of God to guide him "in
ways immemorial." [17] Jesus uses his knowledge of
hearts when he tells Nathanael to follow him, converts
the Samaritan woman, protects the repentant Mary
Magdalen, and tries to rescue the Pharisees from the
consequences of their hypocrisy. When Peter says to
him: "Lord, thou knowest . . . that I love thee," [18]
the word he uses expresses the object of Christ's
knowledge and at the same time that of the Father;
for when the Father knows, he chooses and loves, and
consequently seeks to love.

The bridegroom and the friend

When Christ compares himself to a bridegroom,
he endeavors to show that the Father has the same
tender feeling of love for mankind which a husband
has for his wife. Jave had long ago made it clear that
he intended to behave toward Israel as a husband
would toward his wife. He accuses his people of wan-
tonness and adultery and compares them to a harlot
because of their unfaithfulness: "She is no true wife
of mine, nor I any longer her Lord." [19] Yet he intends
to transform the wanton woman into a faithful wife:
"Everlastingly I will betroth thee to myself, favor and

[16] Ps. 138:2–3.   [18] John 21:17.
[17] Ps. 138:24.   [19] Osee 2:2.

redress and mercy of mine thy dowry; by the keeping of his troth thou shalt learn to know the Lord." [20] God inspires the author of the Song of Songs to describe this ideal union in a work in which the passion of human love is made to serve as a symbol for the mutual love of Jave and Israel: "All mine, my true love, and I all his." "Hold me close to thy heart, close as locket or bracelet fits; not death itself is so strong as love." [21] When Christ shows the tender love of a bridegroom for mankind, he is revealing the sentiments of the Father's heart and consecrates these feelings for all time in the new alliance. He shows that God's love for mankind is characterized, analogically speaking, by all the feelings associated with the love of husband and wife. When Jesus tells his disciples that they ought to rejoice because they have the bridegroom with them and are about to take part in a wedding-feast, he is imparting the joy of the Father to them; for the Father has finally succeeded in wedding himself to mankind through the Son.

Christ also reveals the true mind of the Father when he presents himself as a friend. When he establishes friendly relations with his disciples, Lazarus, Martha, Mary, and the other women, he is carrying out God's wondrous desire to be on simple and familiar terms with mankind. This is what Jave attempted to do shortly after the creation in the garden of Eden; he walked in the garden in the cool of the evening, speaking with Adam and Eve in a friendly

[20] Osee 2:19–20. [21] Cant. 6:3; 8:6.

way. But sin ruined all that. Still, God had a friendly feeling for man in his heart and wished to restore this intimacy. He tries to renew this friendship, broken by original sin, with Abraham. The patriarch is seated at the entrance of his tent during the heat of the day, when he sees Jave suddenly appear before him. Three men are standing there in front of him and Abraham invites them to partake of a plentiful meal. The promise is then made to Abraham that Sara shall bear a child. We have already seen that the friendships of Jesus brought about a complete change in those who were affected. The life of Abraham also undergoes a change, for he becomes the father of a line which will finally give birth to the Messias. This change will also involve a terrible sacrifice for him. We have already seen how difficult it was for Peter to accept the idea of Christ's passion and how he was finally associated with this passion in the manner of his own death. Abraham is also associated in advance with the sacrifice the Father will make of his Son by receiving the order to sacrifice his own son Isaac. God does not spare those whom he loves.

In the account of Jave's relations with Abraham there is another indication of his friendly attitude towards him. "I have made known to you all that my Father has told me; and so I have called you my friends," [22] Jesus tells his disciples. Friendship involves a communication of secret thoughts and mutual confidence. "Should I hide my purpose from Abra-

[22] John 15:15.

ham?" [23] the Lord said to himself; whereupon he revealed to the patriarch his intention to destroy Sodom and Gomorrha. Abraham, on hearing this, appeals in the name of their friendship on behalf of those who are about to be destroyed in the threatened cities. With remarkable boldness he reduces the number of just persons successively from fifty to ten, on whose behalf God declares that he is willing to avert his anger. The patriarch's boldness is finally rewarded with success; Jave yields to his entreaties. Jesus also promises that the prayers of his friends shall be heard.

Other instances of God's friendship for mankind can be found in the Old Testament. A notable case is the encounter of Tobias with the angel. It is God himself who accompanies Tobias on his journeys, cares for him, delivers him from danger, and finally brings him safely back home through the agency of his angel. He is the one who instructs him, gives him advice, and provides him with something to eat and drink. The meal in common serves to promote the Father's friendship with men, just as it does in the case of the Son.

Although the angel Raphael foreshadows the ideal of God's friendship with men, Christ himself is alone able to achieve this ideal. His friendly relations with Peter, John, Lazarus, and the others are much closer and sincere and at the same time more meaningful and sanctifying than all the friendships mentioned in the Old Testament. It would not be correct, however,

[23] Gen. 18:17.

to oppose the latter to the former, for in both cases it is the Father's friendship which is at work. Jesus assures the living presence of the Father's affection in the group of disciples with whom he passes his public life, and the Father accompanies the apostles wherever they go. The familiar love of the heavenly Father, who wishes to share the dwelling place of his Son, is enshrined forever in the hearts of those who, like St. Paul, wish to live in the friendship of Christ.

Benevolence of the Father

There are times when the goodness of Christ assumes a paternal aspect and recalls the affection of the heavenly Father. When he tells his disciples to let little children come to him, they seem to hear the voice of the Father who is anxious to remove all obstacles from the path of those who would approach him. The affectionate way in which Christ embraces and blesses these little ones is expressive of the way in which the Father embraces and blesses them.

The love shown by Christ for the poor and the afflicted is a prolongation of that love which God showed them in the Old Testament. Those who are defenseless and in agony have always been the object of God's care. This is one of the ways in which divine friendship differs from human friendship; the latter is often based upon personal considerations, wealth, or power. God, on the other hand, shows greater concern for those who are poor or unfortunate. When Jesus calls the attention of his disciples to the old woman

283

who has just placed two mites in the temple treasury, he is expressing the admiration of God himself and desires to share this admiration with them. He answers the ignorance and disdain of those who would belittle the woman's action by showing the Father's high regard for what she has done. This regard is what the poor had patiently waited for under the old dispensation. They were vindicated by the fact that God chose to have his Son live in poverty.

The pity which Jesus has for the crowds is a reflection of the great mercy which Jave had for the Jewish people throughout the course of their history. Their history, as a matter of fact, is a prolonged manifestation of the divine mercy. When Jesus notices that many of those who have come into the desert to hear him preach are hungry, he is moved by pity for them, as God formerly had pity on the hungry Jews; and he gives them bread and fish, as generously as manna and quail had been furnished to the Jews in the desert. "And the Lord said to Moses, Their complaints heard, meat for their food at evening, and bread to-morrow to their heart's content; will they still doubt that I am the Lord their God?" [24] Christ simply tells his apostles: "It is for you to give them food to eat." [25] The latter scene has a much more familiar aspect about it, because God has placed himself on a level with men, but the reaction of the Son is the same as that of the Father.

With regard to mercy for sinners, Jesus shows us

[24] Ex. 16:12.   [25] Matt. 14:16.

that his thoughts do not differ from those of the Father. The parables of the prodigal son and the lost sheep illustrate this. The joy of the good shepherd corresponds to the joy of the Father. Jesus describes the eager joy of the shepherd who puts the lost sheep on his shoulders and brings him back home to show all his friends: "Rejoice with me . . . I have found my sheep that was lost." [26] When the prodigal son is seen in the distance, the father runs to him with the same eagerness, embraces him, and covers him with kisses. He says to the servants: "Bring out the calf that has been fattened, and kill it; let us eat, and make merry; for my son here was dead, and has come to life again, was lost, and is found." [27] The same enthusiastic rejoicing is seen in both cases. Nothing indicates clearer than these two parables of the Master the extent to which the heart of the Son is in agreement with that of the Father.

Jesus declares that he has come to save what was lost, and his name indicates that salvation is to come from the Father. "Jesus" signifies "God has saved." Jave himself declared through one of the prophets: "It is I, I, the Lord; no other can bring deliverance." "It was I, ever I, that must be blotting out thy offences, effacing the memory of thy sins." [28] That is precisely what Christ does when he heals the lame man and Mary Magdalen, and when he puts to flight the accusers of the woman caught in adultery. Like the

[26] Luke 15:6.
[27] Luke 15:23–24.

[28] Is. 43:11, 25.

Father and in his name he forgives generously and freely.

Jave not only foretold that men would be saved but referred to the splendor of the Messias' day, when the divine generosity would be made evident on an unprecedented scale. It is just this kind of generosity which Jesus constantly shows by performing countless miracles wherever he goes. When the Master cries to all those who are weary: "Come to me," he is fulfilling the promise of Jave, "who gives the weary fresh spirit, who fosters strength and vigour where strength and vigour is none." [29] His offer to quench the thirst of the Samaritan woman is the echo of a divine prediction: "The water I give him will be a spring of water within him, that flows continually to bring him everlasting life." [30] Jave had said: "I will open springs on the hill-slopes, wells in the open plain." [31] The goodness of the Father always precedes that of Christ and is fully realized in him.

Demanding love

Jesus embodies the thoughts of the Father not only in his benevolence but to an even greater extent in the absolute demands of his love. Ananias is charged by the Lord to say to Paul: "I have yet to tell him, how much suffering he will have to undergo for my name's sake." [32] We are reminded of the terrible trials and sufferings which the prophets were obliged to

[29] Is. 40:29.
[30] John 4:14.
[31] Is. 41:18.
[32] Acts 9:16.

undergo in the Old Testament because God had chosen them. God imposed on them great sacrifices and allowed them to be persecuted; the hostility often shown by the Jewish people to the prophets is recalled by the torments Jesus must suffer. The sacrifice which Christ asks Paul to make is like that which God required from Jonas. Paul was extremely attached to his own nation: "It has ever been my wish that I myself might be doomed to separation from Christ, if that would benefit my brethren, my own kinsmen by race." [33] Jesus sends him among the Gentiles to preach the Gospel, and he is tormented by a feeling of continual banishment and a longing to return, which never entirely leaves him. Jonas also was sent among strangers when Jave commanded him to go and preach to the Ninevites. This mission was so distasteful to him because of his nationalist feelings that he tried to escape by taking a ship for Tharsis. But God discovered these subterfuges, made him obey his orders, and sent him to Nineve. Jonas was obliged to abandon his own people and go to preach among strangers. If Jesus shows that he can be as harsh in the conditions he imposes on those whom he has summoned to follow him, it is because his goodness compels him to insist upon the observance of the same conditions required by the Father.

The Gospel describes for us the great struggle between Christ and Satan; the Old Testament describes God's struggle against the power of evil. The

[33] Rom. 9:3.

account of the temptation in the desert is parallel in certain respects with the account of the fall of Adam and Eve. God curses the serpent and declares endless war on him: "For this work of thine, thou . . . shalt bear a curse . . . And I will establish a feud between thee and the woman, between thy offspring and hers; she is to crush thy head while thou dost lie in wait at her heels." [34] A struggle for the soul of man was thus touched off in the heart of God. This is the fire Christ will bring with him to earth; descended from the woman, he is destined to strike a fatal blow at Satan in the desert, before he wins a final victory over him on the cross.

When Christ looks at the Pharisees in anger, it is the culmination of Jave's anger we are witnessing. How often God had shown his discontent and anger because of the wickedness of his people, endlessly inclined to abandon him and return to their idolatrous ways! How many times he threatened them with dire punishment for their sins and for their disobedience to his law! The exhortations of the prophets are full of threats of vengeance. When Jesus rebukes the Pharisees for their hardness of heart, he is only expressing anew the anger of the Father.

But the object of this anger, like the anger of Christ, is not to punish; it is to warn men and to inspire them with better thoughts. The various signs which show that the anger of Jesus is a form of his goodness are also applicable in the case of Jave. The

[34] Gen. 3:14–15.

book of Jonas describes God's anger with the city of Nineve: "In forty days, Nineve will be overthrown." [35] But his anger is accompanied by sadness and pity, just as Jesus is moved with pity for those who are putting him to death: "And what of Nineve? Here is a great city, with a hundred and twenty thousand folk in it, and none of them can tell right from left. . . ." [36] As soon as the Ninevites begin to do penance, his decision to destroy them is revoked and his anger changed into pity: "When God saw them amending their lives in good earnest, he spared them." [37] Isaias declares: "Leave rebel his ill-doing, sinner his guilty thoughts, and come back to the Lord, sure of his mercy, our God, so rich in pardon." He goes on to say that the thoughts and ways of Jave are infinitely superior to ours: "By the full height of heaven above earth, my dealings are higher than your dealings, my thoughts than your thoughts." [38] What does this superiority consist of? In the fact that God's pardon is always much greater than we should have thought; his threats are only meant to be conditional. What he is really trying to do is to ensure peace and happiness; nothing will prevent him from realizing this purpose. "So it is with the word by these lips of mine once uttered; it will not come back, an empty echo, the way it went; all my will it carries out, speeds on its errand." [39] In the same way when Christ predicts the

---

[35] Jon. 3:4.
[36] Jon. 4:11.
[37] Jon. 3:10.

[38] Is. 55:7–9.
[39] Is. 55:11–12.

end of the world, he gives assurances that all will end with the final triumph of the Son of Man, and he emphasizes: "Though heaven and earth should pass away, my words will stand." [40] The words which will not pass away are those foretelling the final triumph of the Messias. God's anger lasts only for a time; his goodness endures forever.

Although saddened by the hardheartedness of a large number of the Jews, Jesus is consoled by the thought that this obstacle will be the occasion for extending his love to all nations. Jave had already intimated this plan, for he first gave utterance to the thought of Christ: "Claimed my house shall be, for a house of prayer, by all the nations." [41] He likewise decided to show mercy on Nineve, but Jonas rebelled against this divine generosity. The answer of Jave: "Why . . . what anger is this?" [42] and the way he acted on this occasion seem to foreshadow the remarks Jesus will attribute to the owner of the vineyard, when the laborers of the first hour object to the reward paid to the laborers of the eleventh hour: "Must thou give me sour looks, because I am generous?" [43] Father and Son triumph in their struggle against evil because of the generosity of their love.

Gentle and humble heart

We are inclined to think of a gentle and humble heart as an attribute of Jesus rather than of the Father,

[40] Mark 13:31.
[41] Is. 56:7.

[42] Jon. 4:4.
[43] Matt. 20:15.

but Christ reveals the Father in his gentleness and humility.

His retired life in Nazareth for thirty years and his two years of public life remind us of the humility of the Father, who hid himself for thousands of years in the course of man's history, nourishing plans of salvation in his heart and only revealing them after a considerable lapse of time. There is a certain analogy between the thirty years of Christ's obscurity and two years of public ministry on the one hand, and the immense period during which God preferred to remain largely unknown and the comparatively short period of his revelation on the other. The comparison suggests the importance which should be attributed to the Father's act of self-effacement.

Christ has shown us what this self-effacement meant to God. During his years in Nazareth, where he had every opportunity to observe the misery of human souls, Jesus wished to cry out that he was coming to their assistance, but submission to the Father required that he remain silent. The Father also would have liked to proclaim the goodness he had in store for men during all those centuries, but in order to prepare for the Incarnation of his Son and direct men's minds slowly but surely towards this great event, he was obliged to remain silent. He restrained the desire of his heart, accumulating the strength of his mercy from generation to generation, until it could all burst forth in one generous effort.

The patience of Jesus with regard to the failure

of his disciples to understand the true meaning of his teaching recalls the patience of Jave with his chosen people. The assistance which Jesus requires from them in helping him to found his kingdom while leaving the glory to them is an extension of the assistance which Jave required from the prophets in helping him to bring his message before the people while remaining in the background himself.

The tender concern which Jesus shows for the material wants of his disciples reflects the care of the Father, who is equally concerned with the smallest details and desirous of showing his love for mankind by taking care of his humblest needs. Before expelling Adam and Eve from the garden of Eden he makes garments out of skins and clothes their nakedness. During a drought he sends Elias to the river Kerith: "There the river shall provide drink for thee, and the ravens, at my command, shall feed thee." [44] When the river dries up, he commands him to go to a widow in Sarephta and promises to support them both. He aims at providing rest for all when he establishes the obligation of observing the Sabbath. Before Christ placed himself at the service of mankind, the Father had already indicated his desire to help them.

The Father shows a profound respect for human freedom, just as Christ does. The most striking example of this is the Annunciation. After greeting Mary, the angel asks her consent to the divine plan for the salvation of mankind. The collaboration of Mary

[44] III Kings 17:4.

was extremely important if this plan was to be realized, and it would have been logical to suppose that God would bring pressure to bear to ensure its success. But he refuses to do so and allows the Blessed Virgin complete freedom of action with regard to her decision. The execution of his plan is made to depend upon the simple consent of a young virgin.

Jave appears to act in this case, as Christ very often does on many later occasions. Jesus frequently delights in transforming an initial feeling of fear into an expression of relief or joy. After causing anxiety to the woman who touched the hem of his garment, he reassures her by saying: "Go in peace." [45] The greeting of the angel at first troubles the soul of Mary, but the Lord calms her by having the angel repeat the words he had so often used to reassure the Jewish people: "Do not be afraid." [46] The fears of the Blessed Virgin immediately give way to joy and contentment. The Father delights in surprising mankind, just as the Son does.

The simplicity of Jesus is symbolized by his action in taking the blind man by the hand and leading him out of the village before healing his sight. This friendly act is typical of Jave's constant attitude towards Israel, leading it by the hand towards the discovery of his light.

The sacrifice

Finally, the love of the Father can be seen in the love which induces Christ to sacrifice himself for us,

[45] Mark 5:34. [46] Luke 1:30; cf. Is. 12.

because the real initiative for the passion lies with the Father. He is the one who sends his Son to his death and sacrifices his own paternal heart for the sake of mankind: "He did not even spare his own Son, but gave him up for us all," [47] according to St. Paul. If it is true that Jesus offers up to the Father superabundant reparation on the cross for the offenses of mankind, it is not less true that the Father in a certain sense is the first to sacrifice his dearest love. He does not hand Christ over to be sacrificed for his own pleasure. In former times Abraham had shown that he was prepared to strike at himself in the person of his son by "not sparing" Isaac and leading him to the sacrificial block. The patriarch was spared from having to make the sacrifice on this occasion, when God provided a means of realizing it in keeping with his Father's love. Was the Father not the first to feel how cruel the abandonment was to which he had condemned his Son? Could he have looked on coldly or impassively, while the one whom he loved above all else was trembling in the garden of Gethsemani? Could the painful scene at Calvary, which brought so many tears to the eyes of Mary, have failed to touch his fatherly heart?

That is why the artists of the Middle Ages, in picturing the passion, represented the Father with arms outstretched behind the cross. The Father is moved first and last by his love for mankind. He could never have wished for a spectacle such as this but for his great thirst for souls. This is shown by the cry of Jesus

[47] Rom. 8:31.

294

on the cross. Like Christ and by means of him, he "loved his own to the very end." [48]

Perfect image

The heart of Christ is the perfect image of the heart of the Father in all that makes it sublime and heroic, gentle and loving. We are sometimes inclined to believe that Jesus loves mankind with greater warmth and feeling than does the Father, who prefers to remain aloof. This is the mistake of the rich young man and we have seen that Christ rebukes him for his attitude: "God is good, and he only." [49] To prevent us from making the same mistake, he keeps repeating over and over again that the Father loves mankind and that he has received all things from the Father. He is a complete and visible expression of the Father. We have noticed some of the ways in which the various acts of Jesus resemble those of Jave under the old dispensation, but there is an even closer and more essential resemblance in the fact that each act of Christ is related not only to the previous acts of God but to an actual attitude on the part of the Father, results from this attitude, and manifests it. It is the Father who constantly pours forth his goodness in Christ. There is nothing in the love of Jesus for mankind which does not derive immediately from the love of the heavenly Father. No discovery can be more thrilling than that of the heart of the Father in the heart of Christ.

[48] Cf. John 13:1.   [49] Matt. 19:17.

A NOTE ON THE TYPE

IN WHICH THIS BOOK WAS SET

This book has been set in Electra, a type face created in 1935 by W. A. Dwiggins, the well-known Boston artist. This type falls within the "modern" family of type styles, but was drawn to avoid the extreme contrast between "thick and thin" elements that marks most "modern" type faces. The design is not based upon any traditional model, and is not an attempt to revive or to reconstruct any historic type. Since its birth, Electra has met with success because of its easy-to-read quality. This book was composed and printed by the York Composition Company, Inc., of York, Pa. and bound by Moore and Company of Baltimore. The design and typography of this book are by Howard N. King.